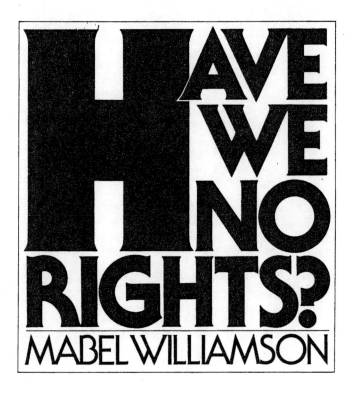

HAVE WE NO RIGHTS?

MABEL WILLIAMSON

Wipf & Stock
PUBLISHERS
Eugene, Oregon

Wipf and Stock Publishers
199 W 8th Ave, Suite 3
Eugene, OR 97401

Have We No Rights?
By Williamson, Mabel
ISBN 13: 978-1-59752-873-3
ISBN: 1-59752-873-0
Publication date 8/10/2006
Previously published by Moody Press, 1957

Contents

NOTE: Most of the Scripture quotations have been taken from the American Standard Version.

Foreword

The book you hold is one many people should read. But I confess to being a bit doubtful whether I can adequately commend it to our contemporary Christian generation. It is not that the book is lacking. Rather, we are lacking. Or, to put it in other words, we are so preoccupied with ourselves and our rights that a book whose central theme is that we have no rights is bound to be unappealing.

It should be read anyway, as I trust it will be. A decade or two ago a popular writer termed ours "the *me* generation," but there is some evidence that this attitude that characterized the 1970s and perhaps even the 1960s is beginning to wane. Some can see that living for self is not the way to happiness. Margaret Halsey recently wrote an article for *Newsweek* magazine entitled "What's Wrong With Me, Me, Me?" in which she strongly warned about America's preoccupation with the self. She warned that people's "search for identity" is bound to fail for the simple reason that identity is not something found but something made through hard choices, work, and commitments to others.

Mabel Williamson is saying the same thing in *Have We No Rights?* But she is doing it on a spiritual and much profounder level attained in part as the result of her many years of service in China as a missionary with the China Inland Mission. Primarily she has young missionaries in mind. She wants to

5

prepare them for the demands of difficult work and the expectations of people operating in a different culture.

Yet her chapters speak to every Christian who is serious about following the Lord Jesus Christ and does not want preoccupation with self to ruin his or her witness to others. The chapters build in intensity, and there can hardly be anyone anywhere who can read this little volume without having one or more chapters strike home in a most disturbing way: "The Right to What I Consider a Normal Standard of Living," "The Right to the Ordinary Safeguards of Good Health," "The Right to Regulate My Private Affairs as I Wish," "The Right to Privacy," "The Right to My Own Time," "The Right to a Normal Romance, If Any," "The Right to a Normal Home Life," "The Right to Live with the People of My Choice," "The Right to Feel Superior," "The Right to Run Things." I cannot even read those titles without sensing how radically different is this standard from most of the basic values of American society and how much Mabel Williamson's book calls us to go beyond even "the simple life-style."

As this book is reissued I would like to record some predictions. I do not believe it will make any list of the most significant books in this or any other year. I do not believe it will be cited by many Christian leaders as "one of the ten most influential books in my life." But even though no one will say that, I believe that is precisely what *Have We No Rights?* is. It is one of the most significant Christian books you will ever have opportunity to read. And if you buy it and take it to heart, I think you will find it to be most influential in your life, as it has been in mine.

James Montgomery Boice

CHAPTER 1

Rights

WELL," SAID MOTHER, setting down a cup she had just wiped, and picking up another, "the older I get, and the older my children get, the more I realize how little right a person has even to her own children. By the time they get—well—into high school they aren't yours any more."

"But, Mother," I protested, dropping a dripping dishcloth into the dishpan and looking at her in amazement, "of course we are yours! Whose else would we be?"

There was silence for a moment. Then, "You— you belong to yourselves," she said quietly.

America—the land of freedom and opportunity! The land where everyone's rights are respected! The land where the son of a shiftless drunkard can grit his teeth and say, "I'm going to be rich and famous some day!" Here in America we pride ourselves on the fact that everyone has the right to live his own life as he pleases—provided, that is, that he does not infringe upon the rights of someone else.

7

Rights—your rights; my rights. Just what are rights, anyway?

A group of half a dozen missionaries were gathered for prayer in a simply furnished living room of a mission house in China. For a few minutes one of the group spoke to us out of his heart, and I shall never forget the gist of what he said.

"You know," he began, "there's a great deal of difference between *eating bitterness* [Chinese idiom for "suffering hardship"] and *eating loss* [Chinese idiom for "suffering the infringement of one's rights"]. 'Eating bitterness' is easy enough. To go out with the preaching band, walk twenty or thirty miles to the place where you are to work, help set up the tent, placard the town with posters, and spend several weeks in a strenuous campaign of meetings and visitation—why, that's a thrill! Your bed may be made of a couple of planks laid on sawhorses, and you may have to eat boiled rice, greens, and beancurd three times a day. But that's just the beauty of it! Why, it's good for anyone to go back to the simple life! A little healthy 'bitterness' is good for anybody!

"When I came to China," he continued, "I was all ready to 'eat bitterness' and like it. That hasn't troubled me particularly. It takes a little while to get your palate and your digestion used to Chinese food, of course, but that was no harder than I had expected. Another thing, however"—and he paused significantly—"*another thing* that I had never thought about came up to make trouble. I had to 'eat loss'! I found that I couldn't stand up for my rights—that I couldn't even *have* any rights. I found that I had to give them up, every one, and that was the hardest thing of all."

That missionary was right. On the mission field it is not the enduring of hardships, the lack of comforts, and the roughness of the life that make the missionary cringe and falter. It is something far less romantic and far more real. It is something that will hit you right down where you live. The missionary has to give up having his own way. He has to give up having any rights. He has, in the words of Jesus, to "deny himself." He just has to give up *himself*.

Paul knew all about this. If you do not believe it, look at I Corinthians 9. "Have we no right to eat and to drink?" he asks. "Have we not a right to forbear working? . . . Nevertheless," he goes on, "we did not use this right. . . . Though I was free from all men, I brought myself under bondage to all, that I might gain the more" (vv. 4, 6, 12, 19).

Paul, as a missionary, willingly gave up his rights for the sake of the Gospel. Are we ready to do the same?

"But," someone will ask, "why should this be especially true for the *missionary?* What rights must be given up on the mission field that a consecrated Christian at home would not have to give up?"

The following chapters picture some of them.

CHAPTER 2

The Right to What I Consider a Normal Standard of Living

"Have we no right to eat and to drink?"
—I Corinthians 9:4

THE WHITE-HAIRED MISSION SECRETARY looked at me quizzically. "Well," he said, "it's all in your point of view. We find that these days in the tropics people may look upon the missionary's American refrigerator as a normal and necessary thing; but the cheap print curtains hanging at his windows may be to them unjustifiable extravagance!"

My mind goes back to a simple missionary home in China, with a cheap rug on the painted boards of the living-room floor. I can see country women carefully skirting that rug, trying to get to the chairs indicated for them without stepping on it. Rugs, to them, belonged on beds, not on floors, and they would no more think of walking on my rug than you would on my best blanket! I think of our dining table set for a meal, and visitors examining with amazement the silver implements instead of bamboo chopsticks; and white cloth instead of a bare table. I

11

think of having overheard our cook say proudly to a
chance comer, "Oh, of course they have lots of money!
Why, they always eat white bread; and they have
meat every day, nearly; and as for sugar—why, you
just can't imagine the amount of sugar they use!"

English service was over, and we went home with
a lady doctor and nurse of another mission. They
had invited us to Sunday night supper. The sermon,
delivered by a missionary of still another mission, who
was stationed in the city, had been striking and
thought-provoking. The text had been Luke 8:14:
"And that which fell among thorns are they, which,
when they have heard, go forth, and are choked with
cares and riches and pleasures of this life, and bring
no fruit to perfection."

"This verse must refer to missionaries," the speaker
had begun, "because it says that when they have
heard, they go forth."

He had gone on to describe a picture he would like
to paint. All around the border were to be the "cares"
and "riches" and "pleasures" that hindered the real
work of the missionary. Subjects that hit home were
mentioned—there would be a big account book that
tied the missionary down so that he had no time for
a spiritual ministry; a teacup, symbolizing the round
of entertaining that may develop in a city where there

is a relatively large missionary community; a house
and its furnishings, needing constant attention; and
so on. The conclusion of the sermon had been very
solemnizing, because of all these cares and pleasures
and things that are second to God's best, it is tragical-
ly possible that the missionary may "bring no fruit
to perfection."

At the supper table we had an interesting discussion of the sermon and its implications. Then the
lady doctor made a remark that I have never forgotten.

"When Frances and I set up this house," she said,
"we agreed that one principle must never be violated.
We would have nothing in our house—its furnishings its arrangement—nothing that would keep the
ordinary poor people among whom we work from
coming in, or that would make them feel strange
here."

A standard of living—what does it amount to?
How important is it? Does it matter whether we missionaries sleep on spring beds, or those made of boards
(I prefer the latter myself!), whether we eat with
chopsticks, or fingers, or forks; whether we wear silk
or homespun; whether we sit on chairs or on the
floor? Does it matter whether we are poor or rich?
Does it matter whether we eat rice or potatoes? Does

it matter whether we live in the way to which we are accustomed, or adopt the way of living of those to whom we go?

It may matter quite a lot to ourselves. Most of us like potatoes better than rice. That is to say, most of us like things the way we are used to having them rather than some other way. What is to be our attitude on the mission field? Are we free to try to have things the way we would like them, and to live, as much as possible, as we would at home? Or ought we to attempt, as far as we can, to conform to the way of life of the people among whom we live? This, of course, brings us to other questions: Does it matter to the people to whom we go whether we conform or not? And, more important, does it matter insofar as the progress of the Gospel is concerned? Will our conforming help to win souls to Christ?

The first thing to be said in answer to these questions is that the standards of missionary living necessarily must vary with local conditions. In some places there is a mixture of races and peoples, each in general keeping with its own customs and dress, and yet mixing freely with the others. In such places there may be many Westerners, and Western ways may not only be familiar, but even adopted to a certain extent by the local people. In situations like this there may be little or no need for the missionary to change his ordinary way of life.

Most missionaries go to places where the way of life is different from their own, and to people to whom their way of life is strange and by whom it is not understood. It is natural for us to like people who do things in the way in which we like them done. We are attracted to those who seem the same as ourselves, and turn (perhaps unconsciously) from those who seem queer and different. People of other lands are the same. When we see someone whose complexion, features, clothing, language, manners, and customs are different from our own, our natural reaction is to stare, or laugh, or both. It is not natural to be attracted to those who are different from ourselves. The missionary wants to attract people. People must be attracted to him before they can be attracted to his message. They must accept him before they will accept his message. The more we can conform to their way of life, the easier and more natural and more rapid their acceptance of us will be.

The report of a China Inland Mission conference of missionaries held in England a few years ago includes as one of the lessons learned from past experience of missionary work in China, "the will to conform as nearly as possible to the social and living conditions of the people to whom we went." This means, of course, that different missionaries will live according to different standards. For example, my sister Frances and I are both members of the China Inland Mission. During the past few years I have been living in the modern and wealthy city of Singapore. I lived according to an ordinary middle-class standard —which meant running water, electricity, gas, and modern plumbing. I was conforming to the social standards and living conditions of the people to whom I went. During the same time my sister was in the Philippines, living in a palm-leaf hut in a clearing in the jungle, carrying her own water and sleeping on the floor. She was conforming to the social standards and living conditions of the people to whom she went. Paul says: "I am become all things to all men, that I may by all means save some" (I Cor. 9: 22). He found what the present-day missionary finds, that to some extent he must adopt the way of life and the standard of living of the people to whom he was sent.

Now, in what measure will it be desirable to adopt the local way of life? What principles will guide us? Well, in the first place we will certainly want to become familiar enough with it so that we feel at home in their homes. If we find their way of sitting uncomfortable, and their food unpleasant, they are not going to enjoy having us as guests. I may think it disgusting to eat my rice off a banana leaf with my fingers, but if I show that disgust, I probably will not be invited again. And my hostess may decide that I am merely an unmannerly foreigner, and that there is no profit in pursuing my acquaintance, or in listening to the strange stories of Someone called Jesus that I am so fond of telling. It is also in their homes that we may become really acquainted with them, and learn to know their needs. When we have become familiar with how they eat, how they sleep, how they work, how they play, what they like, what they dislike, what they hope, what they fear, how they think, how they feel—when we really understand them, then, and only then, will we be able to present the Gospel to them in an adequate way.

In the second place, we will want to live in our own homes on the mission field in such a way as to make our neighbors feel at home when they come to call on us. The fundamental attraction will not be externalities and material things. Even though I live in a little hut that is identical with their own, if in my heart I just do not like to have them around, they will know it, and they will not be attracted to me. But if not only the love and the welcome are there, but also a way of life that corresponds to their own, the approach will be made still easier.

This does not mean, of course, that I will unthinkingly accept all local standards. If I go to Central Africa, I probably will not decide that wearing clothes is an unjustifiable luxury. There is no need for me to neglect to sweep the floor of my palm-leaf hut just because my neighbors do not sweep theirs. The fact that everyone else chews betel nut, or plays mah-jongg, does not mean that I will take up these practices. But I will want, as far as possible, to live the sort of life that it would be suitable for a native[1] Christian to imitate.

Another point must also be considered here. We missionaries might voice it like this: "I would love to live as the native peoples do, if I only could; but I just can't take it!" It is true that we may not be able to live entirely as they do and keep our health. The man who was born and bred in the tropics finds the climate just what he likes. The same climate takes all the energy out of the missionary who has come from the temperate zone. Foreigners are more susceptible to local diseases than natives. If the missionary eats only what the local people do, his health may break down. If he himself does all the household chores in a land in which there are no modern conveniences, he may find that he has very little time left in which to study

---

[1]This word is not used in any disparaging sense, but simply meaning "originating in a given place."

the language or preach the Gospel. On most mission fields it is found that a certain amount of variation from the local mode of life is necessary if the missionaries are to continue in good physical and mental health.

We can, however, gradually get used to unfamiliar things. I remember once, after I had been in China a few years, visiting a neighboring mission station. New workers had arrived there, a young couple fresh from language school. I was eager to meet them, but they did not appear. In answer to my inquiry, the reply was, "Oh, they were invited out to a feast last night, and it's upset them both! They are both in bed!"

My heart sank. Whatever use will these young workers be, I thought, if they can't eat Chinese food? They won't be able to go to the country and minister in all the little country churches that are so much in need of help—they can't get Western food there! They had better have stayed at home!

After a few years had passed, however, the young man mentioned above did start to do country work, and he did it very acceptably. What is more, he even came to prefer an ordinary country meal of local food to the best Western dishes that his wife could give him at home! Seeing that, I began to realize a thing that should be a comfort to all young workers who find the food or the living conditions difficult. *Over a period of time familiarity not only turns difficulty to ease, but often even removes the "dis" from dislike!*

The young worker goes with an older one to make a call or two. Everything is new. Everything is strange. Everything is nerve-wearing. If a seat is offered, it is uncomfortable. If food or drink is offered, either may be unpleasant. Even if he understands more or less of what is being said, the conversations are tiring. And by the time he reaches home he is utterly worn out. As far as he is concerned, however, that is not the worst. He looks at the older worker who has taken him out—someone getting on in years, perhaps a bit stooped, and obviously not in the pink of health. This missionary has done all the younger one did, and more. He also preached a few times to crowds that gathered, and he carried on endless conversations, but just listening made the younger worker tired. Yet this older man somehow has arrived home as fresh as a daisy!

The new worker, in his first station, often has to go through a stage in which he finds everything uncomfortable, unattractive, and difficult, but there is no need for him to become discouraged. Even that older worker probably did too, although he may have forgotten it! The change comes slowly, and the young missionary may not be able to see it for a long time,

but if he everlastingly keeps at it, he will surely find
that, after a few years, familiarity has made the difficult easy. Most people will find, as well, that it has
even made the distasteful pleasant!

A mother was coaxing her little daughter to eat her
vegetable. "But I don't like it!" the child objected.

"But you will," encouraged the mother. "Just eat
it a few times and you will get used to it. It won't be
long before you really like it!"

The child sat stock-still for a moment, considering.
Then she burst out, "But I don't *want* to like the hor-
rid stuff!"

Other people's ways, other people's customs, other
people's standards—do we *want* to like them? Or do
we cling tenaciously to our own, insisting that they
are the only good and right ones? It is the attitude of
mind and heart that matters. If we are willing to give
up our own standard of living, willing to live as far
as possible according to someone else's standards, then
surely it is the business of our Master to make that
possible in such degree as He sees is needed and best.
Before we go to the field then, let us give up all right
to our own standard of living, and be ready contented-
ly to embrace, as far as He makes possible, that of the
people to whom He sends us.

CHAPTER 3

The Right to the Ordinary Safeguards of Good Health

"They must count the cost, and be prepared
to live lives of privation, of toil, and perhaps of
loneliness and danger. They will need to trust
God to meet their need in sickness as well as in
health, since it may sometimes be impossible to
secure expert medical aid. But, if they are faithful
servants, they will find in Christ and in His
Word a fulness, a meetness, a preciousness, a joy
and strength, that will far outweigh any sacrifice
they may be called upon to make for Him."
—*The Overseas Manual of the
China Inland Mission
Overseas Missionary Fellowship*
(1955), p. 4.

I CAREFULLY SPREAD a large handkerchief on the
desk to keep my arm from sticking, took up my
pen, and began painstakingly to practice writing the
intricate Chinese characters before me. Every few
minutes I stopped to wipe the perspiration from my
face.

"How about going out to Uncle Wong's with me?"
My sister had come into the room. "The pastor's wife
intended to go with me, but now she has company

and can't go. It will give you a good chance to practice talking Chinese, so the time won't be wasted—as far as your study goes, I mean."

We got our umbrellas, palm-leaf fans, and tract bags, and started off. The sun was beating down, and the temperature certainly was higher outdoors, but the breeze gave an illusion of coolness, and the pleasant country road upon which we soon entered was enough to make up for a little extra heat. The two miles were quickly covered, and we found ourselves greeted effusively by Mrs. Wong and her daughter.

"Imagine you two teachers coming out here today, when it's so hot! We are entirely unworthy of such consideration! Why, you might make yourselves ill, not being used to such heat in your honorable country! Do sit down and rest! This bamboo bed here in the shade of the house is a cool spot. Daughter, get the teachers fans. Oh, you have brought them with you! Yes, fans are indispensable in this weather! Quickly start the fire, daughter, and heat water for tea! Oh—" a sudden thought struck her, "we have no tea leaves in the house! Daughter, you run to the neighbors and borrow some. Don't go to any of these folk nearby. They are all poor and probably wouldn't have any. Go to Fourth Aunt's, over in the other end of the village."

At home we always kept a crock of cooled boiled

water on hand, but here there was nothing like that; and drinking unboiled water was as unthinkable to her as it was to us. We protested vigorously that we would just as soon have "white tea" (boiling water) as tea made with leaves, but Mrs. Wong would not hear of such a thing. Suddenly an idea struck her.

"Oh," she said, "I know something much better! Daughter, just run to the garden and pick some cucumbers! They'll be better than hot tea anyway, and quench one's thirst just as effectively."

The daughter ran off. After a few minutes the big son came along with two brimming buckets of cold well water and poured it into the stone water butt, which had been almost empty. "Do you prefer to wash your faces in cold water or hot?" Mrs. Wong asked.

"Oh, cold, please!" we both replied, already feeling in anticipation that cold water on our hot faces; but Mrs. Wong, conscience-smitten, was already light-ing the fire. "Oh, I shouldn't have asked such a fool-ish question!" she rattled on. "Of course cold water won't remove perspiration. No, no, it's no trouble. It will be warm enough in just a minute."

The hot water was ladled into the basin, and Mrs. Wong looked inquiringly around the room. I poked my sister. "She's looking for a washcloth," I whispered in English. "Quick, tell her we have one, or she'll be putting their already used one in!"

Fortunately the family washcloth hadn't been discovered by the time ours was produced; and we proceeded to wash. I, being the younger, dutifully allowed my sister to use the water first. "Don't wash too close around your eyes," said my sister in an aside to me. "Someone in the family might have sore eyes, and there might be germs on the basin."

After we had finished with the basin of hot water, Mrs. Wong took advantage of it, having found her own washcloth in the meantime. Just at that moment the daughter returned with her apron full of cucumbers, and politely offered a large one to my sister. Her mother quickly snatched it away.

"As big a girl as that, and you don't know anything about hygiene!" she reproved, sternly. "You haven't even washed them!"

As the cucumbers were being washed with the cold well water, I thought to myself that they were probably no more germ-free after the bath than before. Unboiled water from shallow wells is not necessarily free from germs. I said nothing, however. After the daughter had finished scrubbing the cucumbers, the mother got a knife and carefully peeled two big ones. Then she handed them to us. Her own she did not bother to peel.

"We Chinese are very unhygienic," she apologized. "Of course *you* wouldn't eat cucumbers without peeling them!"

What would she have thought if she knew that to our minds neither the washing in cold water nor the peeling made them safe to eat? I glanced at my sister, who was usually very particular about seeing that all raw fruits and vegetables were scalded before eating, and was astonished to find that she was placidly and unconcernedly munching her cucumber. She and Mrs. Wong were already striking up a lively conversation about something else. I followed her example, and found the cucumber very refreshing.

"How can you be so particular about scalding things at home, and then go out to the country and eat unscalded cucumbers?" I asked, as we were wending our way home.

"Oh, we couldn't possibly offend Mrs. Wong by refusing to eat what she had to offer us!" was my sister's reply. "We certainly ought to be as particular as we can when we are in our own home; but when we are guests, and it's a question of offending someone—well, I think the Lord looks after those cases!"

Teacups! Beautiful Kingtechen china of the thousand-flower pattern, thin and exquisite; or perhaps just a rough earthenware cup, with the handle miss-

ing. Everywhere we went in China we found teacups.
Everywhere we went the first thing we were offered
was a cup of tea. Fragrant tea, bitter tea, hot tea, cold
tea; tea served in hand-painted china, tea in an earthenware bowl—whatever the cup was, we lifted it to
our lips and drank. What was the first thing we
thought of as we tasted the tea? Whether it was pleasant or otherwise? The kindness of the one who
offered it to us? Or the dangers that might lurk on
the edge of that cup? For tea, even very hot tea, cannot be expected to sterilize the rim of the cup; and
who knows who used it previously, or what dangerous disease he might have had? It had been washed,
of course, or at least rinsed out, but—

"Don't the Chinese scald their dishes when they
wash them?" you ask. Well, do you? "M-m-m, not
always, but the danger is much less in America," you
say. That may be true; but it is hard to realize the
danger of infection in one's own home, wherever it
may be; and even those who live under what we
might call unhygienic conditions are no more conscious of the danger in their own homes than you are
in yours. I used to think, sometimes, that the most
dangerous thing we met with in China was just an
ordinary teacup, and that the germs that lurked on its
rim were more menacing than tigers or bandits. (Let
me hastily add that in all my fifteen years in that

country, and having partaken of tea from ten thousand teacups, more or less, in many places and in many homes, I am still quite alive, and in good health and spirits!)

"Now, that wouldn't worry me!" you think cheerfully. "I'm just not particular!"

I am sorry, but that is not at all the conclusion I want you to draw from the above remarks. I am giving no one license for not being careful. No child of God should feel at liberty to disregard what he knows to be the rules of good health, just because he feels like it, much less the man or woman on the mission field.

The cook comes in with a basket of foodstuffs fresh from the market. The young missionary spots a particularly luscious plum, picks it up, and takes a bite.

"Mary!" a scandalized senior gasps. "*Whatever* are you thinking of? Eating that plum without scalding it first! You'll likely get cholera or typhoid and die!"

Yes, in most mission stations the rules of hygiene are adhered to very strictly, and it would be a hardy junior worker who could come through alive without observing them.

Perhaps several years have gone by. You are in charge of the home yourself, and the "discipline" re-

laxes a bit. Perhaps you even resort to washing your
fruit in cold boiled water instead of scalding it, because scalding does spoil it so! Then the younger
workers are sent to you, and you become the head of
a new family. One day, suddenly, one of them gets a
violently upset stomach. Is it cholera? The nearest
hospital is two days' journey away. You catch your
breath, and go ahead caring for her the best you can
with your limited medical knowledge, a constant cry
going up from your heart to the only One who can
help, to Him who is the only all-sufficient One! If
you are fortunate your junior recovers. From that
time on, all the fruit that appears on your table will
be thoroughly scalded.

This is not a chapter on missionary health. It does
not purpose to instruct you in the rules of hygiene.
Rather it inquires into attitudes. Is the missionary to
be as particular as he can about everything (fussy,
some may call it), or should his faith be great enough
so that he overlooks the rules of the doctors? Or perhaps, are there times when the one attitude is desirable, and times for the other?

The Lord of the harvest has sent us forth. A dead
laborer, or even a sick one, is not much use. It is
surely our duty to take all sensible precautions, and
whenever possible to use the safeguards to health

with which modern science has provided us. We have no right at all to disobey the rules of hygiene just because we happen to feel like it. But on the other hand, when those among whom we are ministering, people whose training is different from ours, who have no conception of modern hygiene, out of the love in their hearts provide us with things to eat and drink, surely then is the time to say with Paul, "asking no questions for conscience' sake" (I Cor. 10:27). Surely in cases where adhering strictly to the rules of hygiene would hinder the fulfilling of our commission, we can trust the One who sent us forth to look after us.

CHAPTER 4

The Right to Regulate My Private Affairs As I Wish

"Wherefore, if meat causeth my brother to stumble, I will eat no flesh for evermore, that I cause not my brother to stumble."— I Corinthians 8:13

PLEASE, TEACHER," said a voice at my elbow, "wouldn't you like to wash your face?"

We were having a week in the country. For the fifth time that day, our first full day out, there stood the pastor's wife, holding out to me a basin of steaming water. She had just the right combination of humility and pride in her manner. I quickly stifled the desire to say, "I don't want to wash! What in the world do I want to wash my face five times a day for?" Then I mumbled thanks, and reached wearily for my washcloth. But a little later I tackled her about it.

"Do you always wash your face as often as this?"

"Why, of course!" was the quick reply. "All clean people do! And I was brought up in a very clean family."

33

I let the matter drop, and washed my face (and my feet) as often as she thought best for the rest of the trip.

Grandmother Bay's little granddaughter had just come back from Shanghai. Grandmother Bay proudly appeared at church accompanied by a prettily dressed, well-behaved child of about nine. After the service several of us sat chatting. One old lady looked at the child's pretty frock, and then gave a quick glance at her grandmother.

"I suppose that's the Shanghai style," was all that she said, but Grandmother Bay divined her meaning.

"Just what I thought myself!" She quickly caught up the remark. "It's pretty material, and nicely made —cut a bit closely, but I suppose those Shanghai tailors do it that way. But the sleeves! Practically no sleeves at all! It's almost indecent! But you know, she has hardly a scrap of the material, and I haven't been able to match it. Otherwise I should have lengthened them immediately. It's too good a garment to throw away. I don't know what in the world to do about it!"

I sat listening with my mouth open. The child was little enough so that I would hardly have been surprised to see her running around the yard with nothing on but a pair of trousers, as many smaller girls did. (The boys needed still less!) The objectionable sleeves were just long enough to cover her shoulders. What was wrong with that for a child of her size?

I looked at the two women, trying my best to understand their point of view. What I saw made me gasp. In that area the older women all wore thigh-length loose jackets, and loose trousers, as their regulation attire. It was warm, and one of the two women had just pulled up her trouser legs. Her short stockings reached about eight inches above her ankles, and were held in place by tight round garters. She vigorously fanned her bare knees as the two, with serious, troubled faces, continued the conversation about the "indecent" dress.

What is decency anyway? In certain groups in India it is not decent for a woman to show her face, but her bare feet peep from beneath her long robes. Things that look perfectly all right to us look indecent to someone else; and things that look indecent to us may look perfectly all right to someone else!

A young missionary goes inland to her first station. "I'm not going to look frumpy!" she declares, and takes all her prettiest dresses. When she comes out in gay colors that are not worn in that backward area, or in short sleeves when everyone else has elbows duly covered, her senior missionary attempts to suggest a bit of alteration in her wardrobe. All suggestions, however, are indignantly rejected. She plunges enthusiastically into work with the children, using pictures very effectively to supplement her limited vocabulary. One day her two favorite scholars do not appear, and she asks her helper, a bright high school girl, the reason. The embarrassed and evasive answer does not satisfy, and she keeps after the poor girl until finally she is told the truth. An hour later her senior missionary finds her weeping in her room.

"She said," she chokes, "she said——that their mother won't let them come any more because I—— because I can't be a good woman; I dress like a—a prostitute!"

What is wrong? Why does the eager young missionary have to go through all this heartache? Just because she is not willing to see with someone else's eyes. Her own standards are the only right ones. She learns by hard experience the fact that other people *do* see things differently from us, and that it *does* make a difference. After all, this is their country, and these are their customs. We cannot expect them to adjust to ours. It is the foreigner in the strange land who has to adjust to the ways of that land.

To learn a new language, the ear must be alert to hear just that little turn with which a sound is pronounced that makes all the difference between a foreign and a native accent. To become adjusted to a new people, the eye and the heart must be alert to perceive clearly, to understand and take in their feelings and their reactions. May God grant us the seeing eye and the hearing ear!

"Oh, they're terribly strict at that Bible school!" someone remarks. "There are rules about how long your dresses must be, and how you must wear your hair. I wouldn't stand for it! Why, it's things like that that give Christianity a bad name!"

Perhaps. At the same time, one who has shown that he is willing to give up his own standards and conform to someone else's, even though he may not see the reason for those standards, has shown an attitude that will take him a long way on the mission field. The "how I do my hair and what kind of clothes I wear is my own business!" attitude so frequently met with, both at home and on the field, is not a promising one. If we have fully given ourselves to Christ, nothing is our own business—it is all His.

CHAPTER 5

The Right to Privacy

"There were many coming and going, and they had no leisure so much as to eat."—Mark 6:31

"But when he saw the multitudes, he was moved with compassion for them."—Matthew 9:36

I HAD JUST COME BACK from a strenuous month in the country. Mr. and Mrs. Sprightly, the young married couple who were in charge of the mission station, and I were relaxing around the tea table. I told about the work I had been doing, and answered interested questions. Finally the talk drifted into lighter channels, and Mrs. Sprightly told a funny incident she had witnessed the previous day in a courtyard down the street when she had been out for a walk with her little boy.

"I always like to have Sonny with me when I go out," she concluded, philosophically. "When he's along I can stick my nose in anywhere I like. All I have to do is to say, 'My little boy wants to see what that is,' and I can wander into their courtyards, or even into their houses, and nobody thinks anything about it!"

Curiosity is a common trait, and especially so among those who are uneducated and unsophisticated. Missionaries often find those to whom they go frankly curious. But, strangely enough, there is something in many of us that rebels against having one's private life a matter of common knowledge! The one who has grown up without becoming acquainted with the meaning of the word *privacy,* on the other hand, may find it impossible to understand why the missionary desires to be alone once in awhile!

The young missionary hears the sound of Chinese music from somewhere up the street. To her ears it is weird and unintelligible, but the children at their play instantly recognize the tune, and raise their voices in a shout.

"The new daughter-in-law[1] is coming! The new daughter-in-law is coming!"

A friendly youngster pokes his head in at the missionary's door. "Wouldn't you like to come and see the new daughter-in-law?" he asks politely. "The sedan chair is just arriving. Hurry!"

"But—dear me!" protests the missionary. "Whose home is this new daughter-in-law coming to? Is it a

---

[1] Colloquial Chinese term for a bride.

family we are acquainted with?"

"Oh, *that* doesn't matter!" the boy assures her. "Why, everybody goes to see a new daughter-in-law!"

The missionary, reluctantly allowing herself to be pulled along by the hand, finds it even as the child has said. Crowds of children, and older people too, are swarming in at the open gateway through which has just passed the gaily decorated sedan chair. Though the courtyard is fairly commodious, it is packed with people, talking, gesticulating, pushing to get a better vantage point from which to view the bride when she alights. The groom and his parents are graciously welcoming invited guests, entirely unconcerned about all the hubbub. The bridal chair is set down to a great popping of firecrackers, the appointed welcome committee of several girls and one older woman draws the curtain and assists the bride to her place in the yard, and the ceremony proceeds. After it is completed, the bride is escorted with much formality into the house, and to the bedroom prepared for her, where she is seated upon a bed resplendent with red satin quilts. Then the guests, invited and uninvited, pour into the room. They subject the bride and her clothes to an interested and careful scrutiny, commenting upon everything, with much joking and laughter. As soon as one group gets tired and takes its leave, another is ready to push in and view the "new daughter-in-law."

"The poor girl!" says the missionary. "She looks ready to drop! When will they ever leave her to herself?"

Not until late that night—and the same performance will start again early the next morning. Why, if there were not a continuous stream of visitors for three days, the wedding would be thought rather a flop!

The day had been a busy one. The first visitor had appeared before breakfast, a precursor of a seemingly never-ending stream. There were uneducated country women, whose curiosity could only be satisfied by going through every room in the missionary's house and minutely examining each article that met their eyes. There were those who were educated and formally polite, and dexterously steered the conversation into other channels every time we endeavored to present the claims of Christ to them. There were Christians, some coming with their troubles, others with plans for forwarding the work of the church, and still others with requests for us to set a time when we could go with them to call upon their unsaved friends or relatives.

Finally at four-thirty, after we had ushered out a

couple of callers, we returned, for the first time that day, to an empty room.

"Come, quickly!" I said to my sister. "Let's go out for a walk before someone else comes!" I felt as though I would go crazy if I did not get away—away anywhere, just so it was a place where we could be alone. We hurriedly slipped out the back gate, around the pond, through the back streets, and out the city gate.

"Which way do you want to go?" my sister asked.

"Oh, just anywhere into the country," I said immediately, "where there aren't any people!"

My sister stood stock-still, looking at me in amazement. "Aren't any people!" she repeated. "Aren't any people! *Where* in China do you think you'll find a place where there aren't any people?"

I stood still and looked around me. The flat countryside was dotted with villages, and crisscrossed with paths. Farmers were busy plowing their tiny fields. Coolies in groups of two and three were returning home from the city, scattering in all directions along the many footpaths. People, people everywhere, even out there in the country! These were the people whom I had come to China to seek; yet if I could only get away from them for a few hours! If there were only some wooded gully or mountain thicket where I could be out of sight of everyone! But there were no mountains; the country was as flat as a table-top. I mentally searched the familiar countryside for a place of refuge. Good, fertile land, cut up into tiny fields; well-kept crops, with not a weed any-where; here and there a little grove of trees—surely in among the trees we could be out of sight! But no! There was no undergrowth, no weeds, not even any fallen leaves. All had been gathered, carefully dried, and put in the fuel pile. Why, if a strong wind came up in the night, the owner of the trees would rise from bed and hurry out to sweep up the precious leaves as soon as they fell, just so no unscrupulous neighbor could come and steal them before daylight! And all the lower branches of the trees had long since been trimmed off for fuel. A grove of trees would hide me from the sight of no one, and there was no better place.

The full force of an unpleasant fact suddenly hit me, a fact that I had never before completely realized. There was absolutely no place that I could go to be alone! The best that I could do was to go home to the mission station, into the house, up to my room, and close the door. Even then, who knew how soon someone would call me?

Then, in a flash, a little story I had read in a mag-azine long before came to my mind. A friend dropped in to visit a busy mother. The family was large and poor, and they lived in only one room. It seemed to the vistior that the one room was swarming with children. The mother met her with a beaming face.

"But how can you be so happy," asked the visitor, "when you can never get a minute to be alone? How can you find quiet even to pray?"

"It used to trouble me," was the quick reply, "until I found out the secret. When things get too much for me, I just throw my apron up over my head, and I am all alone with the Lord."

Dear Lord, forgive me! I thought. What about *that* poor mother? And what about the Lord Jesus? He wanted solitude just as we do, and He went with His disciples across the lake to an out-of-the-way spot to be quiet. The multitudes heard where He was going and followed by land. When He stepped from the boat, there were thousands upon thousands waiting for Him. How did *He* react? Was there anger in His heart, or resentment, at never being allowed to be alone? No; for it says that when He saw the multitudes, He welcomed them (Luke 9:11). Dear Lord, give me that same heart of love for the multitudes!

Privacy and solitude are good things, no doubt—in moderation. Most missionaries get less of them than they would desire. There are probably few missionaries who have not been irritated at one time or anoth-

er when their houses and their persons were subjected
to amazed, or delighted, or even half-contemptuous
scrutiny by the curious. *Can't they have the decency
to keep out of what is my own private business?* the
missionary thinks. Yet if we belong to the day, if we
are children of light, why should any act of ours, or
anything belonging to us, need to be hidden in the
dark? This is not to recommend a needless parading
of things that normal people prefer to be reserved
about. Let us remember, however, that people must
come to know us before they can accept our message,
or before our testimony has any value to them. Why
should I desire to keep hidden *anything* that has to
do with myself—*if the sharing of that thing might
help to draw someone to the Saviour?*

> FOR YE WERE ONCE DARKNESS,
> BUT ARE NOW LIGHT IN THE LORD;
> WALK AS CHILDREN OF LIGHT.—
> Ephesians 5:8

CHAPTER 6

The Right to My Own Time

*"Come now, ye that say, Today or tomorrow
we will go into this city, and spend a year there,
and trade, and get gain: whereas ye know not
what shall be on the morrow. . . . For that ye
ought to say, If the Lord will, we shall both live,
and do this or that."*—James 4:13-15

M RS. NING AND I are going out to see Grandma
Woo, who has been sick. Wouldn't you like
to come too?"

I was sitting at my desk, with all the paraphernalia
of Chinese study spread out before me. I looked at
my desk, looked at the clock, looked at my sister, and
then asked, "How soon will you be back?"

"Oh, we shouldn't be too long! Of course Mrs.
Ning walks slowly, with her small[1] feet; but it's only
a mile, and we don't need to stay very long. You
never know, but we ought to be home in plenty of
time for dinner."

Well, I thought to myself, I suppose I ought to go;
but I wanted to finish translating this chapter, and

---
[1]Bound small in childhood.

I'll be doing well to get it done in three hours. And I had thought that I'd get it finished this morning, and be able to write letters this afternoon. Still—

Unfortunately for my peace of mind, I knew two things. One was that my sister thought that I ought to go, and the other was that she was right.

"Well," I said finally, "I'll go; but let's not stay long."

We got our sun hats, joined Mrs. Ning, and started off. Her feet were not more than six inches long, and she *did* take such tiny steps! Try as I would to walk slowly, I continually found myself going ahead of the other two. My sister by nature is in more of a hurry to get things done than I. Still, here she was, wandering along beside Mrs. Ning as if she had all the time in the world, listening intently to a tale about Mrs. Ning's third aunt's cousin, and putting in sympathetic interjections and questions now and then.

I could not seem to get interested in the story, even though Mrs. Ning was telling how she had tried to get this third aunt's cousin to bring his troubles to the Saviour. I could not understand all of what she said, and was unable to keep up with all the ins and outs of the poor cousin's troubles, so finally I gave up trying. It was a beautiful day. The sky was blue, and the wheat, high and greenish-gold, rippled in the wind. We turned off the road and followed a little path running through the wheat fields. My sister almost unconsciously began slipping the full heads of grain through her fingers, one after the other, as she passed. She always loved the wheat, and so did I, but somehow today I did not want to touch it. I only wished that we would hurry.

At last we arrived at the village, and made our way to the home of old Mrs. Woo. As usual, a crowd of dirty, staring youngsters followed us into the house. We sat on benches that were about eight inches wide, and sipped "tea" that could be called so only by courtesy; since, having no tea leaves, they had instead just put a few slices of raw sweet potato into the kettle when it went on the fire. Old Mrs. Woo was up and around again, and feeling lively.

"I'm so glad you've come! I've been telling my neighbors all about the Lord Jesus, and how they ought to believe in Him, but I'm afraid I don't do it quite right. Now that you've come you can tell them! Here, you, Kitten," speaking to one of the crowd of children that had followed us into the house, "you run home and get your grandma to come. And you, Girlie, your second great-aunt said that she wanted to believe. Run fast and tell her that the teachers have come. All of you youngsters, you scoot home as fast as you can and get your mothers and grandmothers to come and listen to the doctrine!"

It took quite a lot of persuasion to get the children to go; and perhaps the mothers and grandmothers were busy. We waited in vain for quite awhile, but finally in came three or four women, one with a cloth shoe sole she was quilting, and another carrying a baby. After quite a bustle, they were all seated and given bowls of tea. Then out came the poster that my sister always carried, and the Gospel was explained to them in very simple words. With great effort I managed to keep my mind on the message, and understood most of it. I congratulated myself internally. At last I had successfully wrested my mind from the absorbing but uncomfortable subject of all the things that I had wanted to get done that day!

The preaching was finished. The women got up to go, assuring us that they would come with Mrs. Woo to church the next Sunday. We got up too, and started to say good-by.

"What! Go home!" said Mrs. Woo. "Who could think of such a thing! Of course you'll stay for dinner with me! Why, it's almost ready!" (We knew perfectly well that the only womenfolk in the family were herself and her daughter-in-law, and that neither had left the room since the tea had been brought in.)

My sister and Mrs. Ning protested, and even I managed to add a few polite words. But my thoughts were not so courteous. Stay for dinner! What an idea!

Why, that would mean that we would not be home before the middle of the afternoon at the earliest! And besides, the meal would probably be some miserable stuff that I could hardly force down! Oh, well, likely she was only asking us in order to be polite, and did not really mean it!

With great difficulty we made our way toward the door. Mrs. Woo and her daughter-in-law hung on us until we could hardly move, protesting loudly that they would not think of letting us leave. My blood began to boil. I guess we had the right to go home when we wanted to! They were actually trying to force us to stay! Well, I would not stay in any case now! This was just too much!

We had reached the open door, and just then caught sight of an old woman hobbling rapidly across the yard toward us.

"Oh, Girlie's second great-aunt!" called Mrs. Woo. "Here you are at last! Why didn't you come sooner?"

"Well, I had company, and I just couldn't get away. But finally my daughter-in-law came back, and I left them with her and came as quickly as I could. I was so afraid that the teachers would be gone. But, oh, surely you're not leaving?"

"Oh, no, of course they're not leaving! You don't think that I would let them come under my roof and not keep them to a meal! It will be nothing like they're used to, of course; but still a meal is a meal! Now, just sit down, teachers, please, and Mrs. Ning. Girlie's second great-aunt has wanted to believe for some time, but her son is very mean to her, and he won't let her go to church. Do you think that she could believe at home?"

I could not believe my eyes. My sister and Mrs. Ning sat down obediently and began to talk very sympathetically with the old woman who had just come. What! Were they actually going to stay to dinner? And not a word to me, just as if what I wanted did not matter at all! *They* could talk to this old lady, and tell her about the Lord, but all *I* could do was just sit! Of course I was supposed to listen; but one could not put her brain to listening to this queer Chinese *all* day long! And what about all those things that I had wanted to get done?

The dinner was no better than I expected. In fact, it was worse. Girlie's second great-aunt stayed too, upon urging, and they all talked on and on. They were trying to teach her a little prayer, and she was so stupid! Over and over and over, and still she could not say it by herself.

Finally, when I had given up all hope—I had sat in stony silence all the afternoon—we got up, made our farewells, and started home. The sun was setting as we entered our front gate. I was tired (why, I did not know; I had not done a thing all day), hungry (I had not been able to eat much of the dinner, no matter how it had been urged upon me), and disgusted. And the worst of it was that it did not seem to bother my sister a particle. She took it all as a matter of course. Was this what I was going to have to go through; what I had come to China for? For I began slowly to realize that today's experience was not just one isolated incident; it was likely to happen any day in the year. Something was wrong somewhere. What?

Suddenly it came over me. It was only that I had had my day all planned out, and did not want my plans interfered with. Because they had been interfered with, I had done nothing but sulk. All the things I might have enjoyed I had not enjoyed at all. I had made myself miserable for a whole day, just because my time had been disposed of by someone else, and not by me.

"Dear Lord," I said, "I'm not going to go through this again! I know it was really You who disposed of my day when I wanted to do something else with it! Give me an open mind, Lord, so that whenever I go to the country, whenever I start a new day, I'll be able to accept whatever comes, and rejoice in it!"

It is amazing how much difference a little thing like one's mental attitude can make. After that, when

I went to the country, I never took with me any pre-conceived notions of what time I would return. I might get back home for my noon meal, or I might get back by sunset, or I might even stay overnight— what difference did it make? My time belonged to the Lord, and it was up to Him to dispose of it. I found that with this attitude of mind I could go anywhere, take advantage of any opportunities offered, stay more time or less time than I had expected, and still enjoy every moment, because God had planned it, and had worked it out in the best possible way.[2]

---

[2]Adapted from *The Lord Stood by Me* (Philadelphia: China Inland Mission, n.d.), pp. 67-75 (out of print).

CHAPTER 7

The Right to a Normal Romance,
If Any

I WAS IN THE CIM MISSION HOME in Vancouver, B. C., an accepted candidate. In two more weeks I was to sail for China, the land where three of my sisters were already laboring as missionaries. One had been out for six years, had been married while on the field, and was almost ready for furlough. The other two sisters had been out a shorter period. They were both single, and stationed together. That day I had received a letter from them written from a little hill resort operated by our Mission, where they and others had gone to escape the worst of the summer heat. Now, for missionaries, a summer resort is the most common place for a romance to develop! The letter was a gay description of their life there, and ended with the following sentence:

"There are thirty-three of us here now: seven married couples with nine children, nine single ladies, and one single man! There is one more single man expected, we hear, but even at that, I'm afraid there isn't much hope for us!"

The dinner bell rang, and I hurried down. But who

was that elderly couple in the old-fashioned clothes? Perhaps I had been told that they were to arrive that day, but if so I had not remembered it. They were introduced all around the circle—missionaries who had just come from China! We sat down, and I found myself beside the lady.

"What did they say your name was?" she asked, apologetically. "I have such a time remembering names."

I told her, and she immediately pricked up her ears. "Williamson!" she said. "Don't you have a sister in China?"

"Yes, I have three there," I replied.

"Well, isn't that a coincidence! When I was in Shanghai I heard—no, you couldn't have heard it yet, for the news was just out—I'm *sure* it must have been your sister! Anyway, just before we left Shanghai there was a great hubbub about the news of a new engagement, and I'm almost certain—Dear," turning to her husband, "who was it that we heard was engaged, just before we left Shanghai?"

Her husband did not remember. "Well, I'm almost sure it was your sister, anyway!" she declared.

"My sister! But it couldn't be!" I replied rather dazedly, thinking of the letter I had just received. "Which one? What was her first name?"

Unfortunately she could not remember that, nor

did she know that there were two Miss Williamsons in China. And as for the name of the man—she had no idea about that, either. The whole thing seemed extremely vague, and altogether unlikely, and I dismissed it from my mind.

A week later I received another letter from my two sisters. To my amazement I read the news that the younger of them had just become engaged to the single man who had arrived at the hill resort the day after the previous letter was written!

After I had partly recovered from the shock, my mind went back to what I had heard of the courtship of my married sister, also in China. The man who later became her husband was stationed at a place a thousand miles from where she was. They had been very slightly acquainted when they were in Bible institute in America, six or seven years before. Suddenly he started writing to her, and after two or three letters, asked her to marry him. When she went down to Shanghai for the wedding, practically all she knew of him was from his letters.

The other sister, who went with her at that time, told me later that when they went to the railway station in Shanghai to meet the expected groom, who did not arrive until the day after they did, she almost had heart failure. After they went to bed that night she could not go to sleep for thinking, "What if she shouldn't want to marry him, now that she's seen him! I'm sure *I* wouldn't!"

Succeeding days set her mind at rest, however, for it was quite evident that the promised bride *did* want to marry him—and so it turned out all right after all!

"What a strange family you come from!" you say. "Your sisters rush into marriage in such a precipitous way!"

No, not at all. Such courtships are fairly common among missionaries. The reason for this is obvious. There is very little opportunity on the mission field for becoming acquainted with eligible persons of the opposite sex. Unless the missionary is prepared to give up his calling in order to marry, his range of choice is necessarily limited to other missionaries; and missionaries, when at work, are usually widely scattered. Most of our mission stations had only one household, with only two, three, or four missionaries. Obviously, it would not be very likely that two single workers of opposite sex would be included in the group; to say nothing of the fact that such an allocation of workers would normally be considered highly unconventional! Usually single women workers were sent to one station, and a man (or men, if there were that many) to another. Missionary travel, except for going to a summer resort, was usually confined to

one's own district, and missionaries working outside
that district met very infrequently.

Another factor that must be taken into consideration is the restriction which local custom puts upon
social mingling of the sexes in heathen lands. Most
missionaries live in near contact with the people, and
it is only right that they should do so. The missionary
who prefers to withdraw from the people is not likely
to make many converts. Local people, both Christian
and heathen, are encouraged to come freely into the
missionary's home, and much of his work may be
done by just such quiet contacts. The missionaries
come in as strangers. They present a new way of life.
Is it any wonder that, as much as is possible, everything that they do is watched? Sometimes the watch-
ing is in order to criticize; sometimes it is in order to
imitate; but always they are watched. If what the
watchers see seems good to them, they may give themselves to the One about whom the missionaries preach.
If they see things that offend them, they may stumble
and turn away. Because of this, local conventions
must be taken into consideration; and in many heathen lands what we would call only ordinary friend-
liness between two persons of opposite sex would be
looked upon not only with disapproval, but even with
suspicion.

Mission rules in regard to such matters are usually

very strict, as the following quotation from *The Overseas Manual of the China Inland Mission Overseas
Missionary Fellowship* (1955) will show!

> It is important that the missionary in his daily
> life among Eastern peoples should maintain a
> standard of dignity and courtesy which is essen-
> tially Christian and not merely Western. It must
> be remembered that a careless disregard of local
> conventions will give offense to nationals whose
> good opinion is of value, and may prove a serious
> hindrance to the progress of the Gospel. Great
> care should be taken particularly by lady workers
> when extending hospitality to missionary brethren
> or *vice versa*, lest any action lead to misunder-
> standing and injury to the work. Engaged couples
> should also be especially careful of their deport-
> ment, remembering that they will be setting a
> standard of behavior for young Christians no
> longer bound by old conventions and looking,
> perhaps, for guidance to their missionary friends.
> . . . Engaged couples will not be designated to
> work in the same center (pp. 21, 22).

So, between the limitation that a narrow circle of
eligible acquaintances sets, and the restriction entailed
in conforming to local custom, young missionaries
may often feel that the chance for any normal kind of
romance is snatched from them. Small wonder that
the summer resort and the post office, the two avenues
of courtship left open to them, are speedily utilized,
and that engagements many times are made on what

would seem at home to be too short acquaintance! If *you* knew that you had only a few weeks in which to become better acquainted and do your courting, and that when those few weeks had passed each would return to his own station, with no opportunity of meeting again for at least another year, perhaps you would speed things up too!

If the choice of a life partner were a matter to be decided purely "on one's own," then this sort of situation on the mission field might lead to many a tragedy. Thank God, that is not the case! After all, He is the One whom we want to make the choice for us, and He can be depended upon. Certainly any young missionary should make this a matter of definite prayer. If God has chosen the two for each other, He will see to it that they meet; and He will bear witness in their hearts as to His leading, so that they need not hesitate or fear. If we set our hearts on some certain thing, irrespective of whether or not it is His will, disaster will result. If we commit the matter entirely to Him, and trust Him to work out His own perfect will, we can go ahead with confidence, knowing that the union (if He indicates it) will be as the path of the just, that "shineth more and more unto the perfect day." If anyone doubts this, let him look at any missionary couple. In spite of all the difficulties and dangers, the percentage of happily married couples must

be greater among missionaries than it is anywhere
else!

To any thinking young person, another problem,
not yet discussed, must be evident. If there are twice
as many single women as single men on the mission
field (and there are), some of the women must either
marry men who are not missionaries, and so leave the
field, or else remain single. The shortage of men on
the mission field is often deplored, and it is true that
in many cases the work would be better off with a
larger proportion of men. I shall always remember,
however, hearing one of my sisters say: "Before I
came to the mission field I thought that the reason
there were more women than men on the field was
that more of the women were wholly consecrated to
the cause of Christ; but after I had been out for some
time I changed my mind. Now I believe that God
calls more women than men because *more women are
needed.*"

The army of unmarried women missionaries on the
field is there, not because there happen to be more
women than men on the field, and, since we do not
believe in polygamy, some were left over; but because
there is a work that they can do that no one else can.
Most men need wives, and the fact that a man has a
wife and family is more of a help than a hindrance in
most types of missionary work. A man missionary can

leave his family for weeks or months, and even though married, he can engage in the arduous itineration that is often necessary. But a married woman missionary, as soon as she becomes a mother, is bound to her children, and that usually means that she is bound to her home. She can engage in missionary work in the place where she lives, but she cannot travel easily. She cannot go out for weeks or months with a women's evangelistic band. She cannot go from church to church, holding Bible classes for the women. In many places, when teams of men workers go about, the women are left almost untouched. There must be women workers to reach the women. There is plenty of work for the married woman missionary to engage in; but there are certain types of work which her responsibilities will not allow her to undertake.

"That's the type of work I want to do!" declares one young woman. "To spend weeks and months in the country villages, living in the people's homes and really becoming one with them—that's the only work that counts! *I* shall never be married."

"Oh," says another, "I'm sure there is much work a married woman can do that would be impossible to the single woman. Anyway, I wasn't cut out for a spinster! It doesn't matter if there *are* only half as many men as women; *some* of the women get married, and I'll be one of the 'some.' "

Well, friends, both of you are wrong. It's not up to you to say what sort of work you want to do, and it's not up to you to say whether you will be married, or one of the single crowd. Since most girls want to be married, it is a good thing for each to face the possibility that God *might,* for a reason, want her to remain single; but that does not mean that I am encouraging anyone to take a vow of celibacy! I know of one young woman missionary who told various fellow workers, and even some of the local Christians, that she was never going to get married. The Lord began to deal with her—at the same time that a young man was laying siege to her heart! She finally surrendered to the Lord, and gave up her cherished dreams of the kind of missionary career she had mapped out for herself. A few years later she was a happy missionary wife and mother!

Most of the above is particularly directed to young women, but it may apply to young men as well. In a limited number of cases it may be necessary for men to remain single, particularly those who engage in pioneer work of a sort that would be impossible for women. This probably means giving up anything that could rightly be called a "home." Even where two single men are together, "batching it" is usually a sorry business; but when the call of the Lord comes, He will give grace. In that respect it is much easier for women. Two unmarried women can live together and make a home that seems like a home; most men do not seem to have that gift!

The advantages and disadvantages of the single woman missionary, as over and against those of the married woman (or vice versa) are often debated. The single woman certainly has the advantage in being able to give all her time and energy to the work, though the married woman can give help to married women in a way that an unmarried woman cannot. It is not a matter for anyone to decide arbitrarily. Remember that "each man hath his own gift from God, one after this manner, and another after that" (I Cor. 7:7). Whatever God has called us to do, we *can* do. Each state has its own blessings. When one sees the "trouble in the flesh" (I Cor. 7:28, K.J.V.) that bringing up children on the mission field entails,[1] it is almost enough to make one feel that the single state is the easier. It *is* easier in some ways, of course. Yet remaining single is not easy either. Every human heart longs for someone to "belong to," and perhaps the hardest thing that the single missionary has to face is that she can never, never say to anyone, "I'm going to stay with you."

---

[1] Cf. ch. 8.

CHAPTER 8

The Right to a Normal Home Life

"After marriage a lady worker continues to be a missionary in active service and her changed status will afford new opportunities for service. She will need rightly to apportion time to language study, home duties and her calling as a missionary. This will require changes in outlook and habits, but if the responsibilities of married life have been prayerfully accepted the varying claims on time and strength will not result in a permanent conflict of loyalties.

"The establishing of a Christian home should be for the glory of God and the spread of the Gospel. One danger to be avoided is that of missionaries becoming so absorbed in their home as to neglect an active ministry amongst the people to whom they have been called. It is the mutual responsibility of both husband and wife to see that each does not hinder the other from fulfilling his or her ministry. Where there are children, it is recognized that new responsibilities are involved, but care should be taken that family claims do not monopolize the time and energies of either parent. Children who grow up in an atmosphere of loving yet firm discipline are not only a joy to their parents but an asset to the work of the Gospel. But when children are over-indulged or uncontrolled, whether on the field or at home, seri-

67

ous harm to God's cause as well as to the reputa-
tion of the Mission may result."

> *—The Overseas Manual of the*
> *China Inland Mission*
> *Overseas Missionary Fellowship*
> (1955), p. 22.

WHAT A WONDERFUL THING is a Christian
home! What a privilege to be able to establish, among thousands of darkened, pagan homes, one
that is truly Christian; and to be able to live out the
love of Christ in actual family relationships before
people who know nothing of it!

This privilege has not been given to me. The Lord
has not led me in that path. And yet, as I have ob-
served many young couples on the mission field, and
older ones too, I have been able to see a little of the
price they have had to pay. The outsider, looking on,
saw only the love and blessing that radiated from
these homes. But as I lived in some of them, I found
that these young couples were faced with constant
problems, and even frustrations, and I wondered
whether or not I could have overcome all obstacles
in the gallant way in which they did.

Shall we take a look at the sort of thing a young
married couple on the mission field has to face? We
will call them John and Mary, and make them just

ordinary folk who meet the kind of situations most young missionaries meet.

A home of her own—that was what Mary longed for. She and John had been married a few months before leaving for the field, had studied for a term in language school, and now were living with an older married couple until their acquaintance with the language and the customs of the people was enough to warrant their being sent to a station of their own. Mary found the language easy, but John found it hard; and they had been on the field for more than two years before their desire for a home of their own was realized. It was just as well for Mary that she was quick with the language. Little David was born when they had been out only a year, and looking after David meant that she had several hours less each day for study than John had.

When they finally got to their new station, they were surprised to find that long, uninterrupted hours for language study, which they still needed, were almost impossible. There was a little church in the place to which they had been sent, and of course they wanted to do what they could, with their limited language, to help. They found a language teacher, but he was not as good as their previous one. Mary had a girl to help her in the house, but she was untrained, and for the first few months Mary thought that it was more work training her than it would have been to do the work herself. They had many visitors, both Christians and others. John loved to sit and talk with the men who came, and although his facility in the use of the spoken language developed, the progress he made in the book work required by the course of study was extremely slow. Mary often longed to shoo the men visitors out the door, lead John into his study, set him down at his desk, and shut him in with his books!

With the care of the baby and the responsibility for the home devolving upon her, it was a good thing that Mary did enjoy study. She often said that she thought the Lord gave her, as a young mother, special help with the language, because He knew how much she had to do! Because she was so busy, however, she often sat up later at night over her books than was good for her health, and she became tired and worn out. The flu came along, and she was an easy victim. Poor John! He had to be nurse, housekeeper, and baby-tender, all at the same time. The thing that worried Mary the most about being ill was that she was keeping John from his studies.

Mary was not entirely back to normal health when David's little sister was born. What a darling she was! Before her illness, Mary had been giving a short Bible talk at the women's meeting every other week; but now it seemed impossible to find time for the hours of preparation such a talk entailed. Because of her slow recovery it was finally decided that she and the children must go to a hill resort earlier than usual that summer. When she returned, she was horrified to realize that it had been six months since she had given a message in the native language.

She was feeling much better in every way, however, and settled down to "get back into the work." The girl who helped her had developed nicely, and now the two children could be entrusted to her care. In spite of John's slowness at the language, he had always been able to make himself understood, and the little church was growing. With his encouragement, they had started a preaching band, and went to nearby towns and villages with the Gospel. Sometimes they stayed away for several weeks at a time. They insisted that John accompany them; and indeed, he would not have been happy anywhere else. But more and more Mary found herself left alone at home with the children. Where was the happy home that she had wanted to establish for John? He was as dear and as kind as ever when she saw him—but he was away so much! And during the times he was at home, there were often visitors to see him. On evenings when there were no visitors she always longed to say,

"Come and sit in the easy chair, John, and we'll have a cozy time together," but her Puritan conscience usually overcame the promptings of her heart, and instead she would look at the clock and say brightly, "Oh, there's still time for you to get in an hour or two of study! Isn't that nice!"

The time passed rapidly. John *did* persevere with his language study, and very slowly got off the required examinations. Mary never had as much time as he did for study, but she usually kept ahead of him in the book work. She did not dream of trying to rival him in his knowledge of the spoken colloquial! At first she used to save up her problems for him to deal with, but she found that when he returned from a country trip he was always so tired that she did not like to burden him, and soon she was struggling alone with most of them. The children grew rapidly, and usually kept in health, although there were several occasions when they had serious illnesses. At such times she would realize afresh that, although the nearest fully qualified doctor was several days' journey away, the Great Physician was always near!

When David was four, two new missionaries, fresh from their term at language school, were sent to be with them—two bright, happy girls, whom Mary welcomed with all her heart. The care of the larger household took more time, but she did not grudge it.

One was quick at the language, and one was slow. When the discouraged one would come with her troubles, Mary would comfort her by telling her that John had been slow too! The two girls became very fond of the children. Mary was almost overscrupulous about not allowing them to disturb the two, who were supposed to be giving all their time and effort to language study. The quick one, Alice, raced through two language exams, and then had a week in the country with the women's evangelistic team (organized a year previously, Mary being one of the chief promoters). It was what Mary had longed to do herself ever since the band was started, but—well, she had her babies! After all, they *were* the most precious children in the world! But when Alice returned, bubbling over with the novelties and thrills of a week in the country (fortunately she was not afflicted with a delicate digestion, and could eat anything with relish —and comfort!), poor Mary had all she could do to "rejoice with them that do rejoice." Afterward, in the privacy of her own room (John was not at home, and the children were asleep), she finally let go, and the sobs came—stifled by the bedclothes, so that the children would not be awakened.

And then it was time for furlough! The homeland seemed strange at first, but they soon got used to things. Everyone was extremely kind, and showered

them with gifts. The meeting with loved ones and
friends was all that they had expected; but the strain
of living with their children in other people's homes
(even though they were the homes of their own dear
ones) made things difficult. The relatives constantly
petted the children, and discipline became a problem.
Finally they were able to get an apartment of their
own for a few months, and David started kindergarten. John was constantly in demand as a deputa-
tion speaker, and he traveled back and forth, speaking in many places. Sometimes Mary thought, with
a sigh, that she saw less of him on furlough than she
had on the field!

Certainly they were having a wonderful time at
home, but still it would be nice to get back to the
field again! Then, with the thought, came a stab of
pain—for she knew that when that time arrived it
would mean sending little David off to school. The
school for missionaries' children was a long way from
their part of the field, and the most they could hope
for after that was to have David during the summers,
and on their furloughs. Her little David! Going so
far from home, among strangers! Perhaps she could
keep him awhile, and teach him at home. If only the
leaders of the Mission were not so strict about insisting that all children of school age be sent to the
school for missionaries' children! What did they

know of a mother's love for her little boy? But before this thought was fully formed, her heart was reproving her. Of course they knew. Most of them had children of their own. It was all for the children's good. She had no training for teaching, and look how busy she had always been! Wherever did she think she would get time to teach David?

Besides, her mind ran on, David needed to be with other children of his own age and race, and to get the "give-and-take" that school life provides. Kindergarten had already been a help. And on the field there were so many other difficulties! While they were still there, she had tried her best not to let David feel that he was different from, or superior to, the children he played with; but she just couldn't let him do all the things that they did. And he had always wanted to know why—why couldn't he wipe his nose on the back of his hand, as all the other children did? Why did he have to go to bed at a certain hour, when all the other children stayed up as long as they wished? She certainly had never said, "It's because you are an American, and we are different," but somehow David had seemed to acquire that sort of attitude, and to feel that he was superior to the local children. She still remembered how helpless she had felt in trying to deal with the situation!

Well, it did seem that sending him away to school

would be necessary if he were not to grow up proud
and overbearing. Then too, she remembered the day
she had to spank him because he had become angry
and shouted at one of his little playmates in very filthy
language. Where had he learned those words? (He
had picked up the language, good and bad alike, without even trying!) She wouldn't even have known
what the words meant, but she had overheard the
Bible woman scolding him, and had gone out to see
what was wrong. The Bible woman hadn't wanted
to tell her, but she would not be satisfied until she did.
No, if her boy was going to learn filth like that by
being inland with her, there was no help for it—he
must go to school. "Dear Lord," she prayed, "You
know what's best, and I suppose he's got to go; but,
oh, Father, it's like tearing my heart out to send him!"

The time came. John and Mary went back to the
field. David went off to school, bravely choking down
the sobs, but with a pathetic, lost look in his eyes that
stabbed his parents' hearts. They tried to forget it,
and to rejoice in the thought of soon meeting again
the dear group of Christians in their old station. But,
no! A sudden call came, an urgent call to a hard
place, in an entirely different part of the field. After
much discussion and prayer, it was settled. There was
no chance to go to their old station, even for a visit.
Soon they were far away, among strangers, living in

two rented rooms, and trying to straighten out a very difficult church situation, the like of which they had never before experienced.

Stories end, but life goes on and on. And the human mind always seems to magnify the present difficulties, and glamorize the possible future. John and Mary thought that they had it rather hard their first term, and that the second would be easier; but when the second term actually began, and they looked back on the first, they thought it had been nothing but child's play!

Looking at that first term objectively, we can see that John and Mary really did have a relatively easy time. For one thing, they lived in only two places all that time. For one reason or another missionaries often have to move time and again. Someone who is doing an absolutely indispensable job breaks down and must go home on furlough, and you are the only one who can take over. Or the work is being expanded, and the older workers are scattered farther afield as new ones come in. Perhaps there is a war, and your station is in the fighting area, and you have to evacuate. Whatever the reason is, suddenly you find yourself in the midst of breaking up your home, packing and moving, and then settling in a new place, finding new people and problems with which to get acquainted, and perhaps a new dialect to learn.

Other things had been comparatively easy for John and Mary too, that first term. They did not have any fellow workers who were "difficult." It was not their lot to start work in virgin territory, or where the people were unfriendly. They did not get into any difficult church situations. The church people were eager to co-operate with them, and quick to profit by their teaching and example. Even in the matter of health, they did not have a more than average amount of illness. And the story of their accomplishments during that first term could truly be used as a model for the young missionary's emulation!

This is not to say that John and Mary had no difficulties. Difficulties are the normal thing on the mission field, and they had their share. But they met their difficulties, and they made good. How? Chiefly by giving up some of their "rights," and foremost among the rights they gave up was their chance for a normal home life. There was rarely an evening when John was at home and without a visitor; and if such an evening came, he spent it at his books. Later he was away from home for days and weeks, so that the home had to function without the father much of the time. John had to give up his right to spend a normal amount of time with his wife and children. Even

Mary could not spend as much time with the children as she would have liked, nor arrange things for them as she might have wished. And then, after the first few years, their home was not theirs alone. Most of the time they had other people living with them. All the way through they had to put the Lord's work first, and their home second.

Yet was not this attitude of self-sacrifice the thing that made their home a real Christian home? If they had put their home first, not the work—if that home had become a self-centered thing, a thing enjoyed for its own sake—would it not have failed to be what they wanted it to be? A home that is absorbed in itself is not a truly Christian home. John was willing to be away so much, and to sacrifice so much, because his love for his Master was the all-consuming passion of his life. It was for exactly that reason that his presence—and even the consciousness of his absence, and the reason for it—did bless that home. John and Mary gladly took others into their home, really wanting them, not because they did not appreciate having their own home to themselves, but because their concern for the work was greater than their natural desires. They counted the cost, and sent their child away from them, away to school, because they knew that it was best for the child and best for the work. Love for Christ was greater than love for home, or for children, and greater even than love for each other. If they had held on to their right to home, and given it first place, that would have meant losing it—losing the Christ-centered home that they wanted. But in giving it up they found it—found a home that truly showed forth the love of Christ, because that love was the compelling force of their individual lives.

away—I may have to live with one that Mr. Gibb picks for me for a year or two—but I'm getting the one I've picked for myself in the end!"

At that juncture two girls jumped upon the speaker, and rolled her from the bed to the floor. "Just because you are engaged you don't need to think you are better than we are!" and the serious discussion broke up with a laugh.

With whom am I going to live and work for the next six months? For the next six years? For the rest of my life? Who will be the one I will see the first thing in the morning, and the last thing at night, and all the time in between? With whom will I sit down at the table three times a day? Who will be my fellow worker, my companion in recreation, the one who spends time with me at the Throne of Grace, pleading for souls, and for the upbuilding of God's Church? Yes, it's quite a question. For somehow, mission boards usually seem to recognize only one legitimate reason for allowing a missionary to choose his or her own fellow worker, and that one reason is marriage. Even married couples will probably be asked to take one or more younger workers into their homes; and if you are one who remains single, why, you will just have to let the superintendent, or com-

mittee, pick your companion and fellow worker for
you.

When I was in high school it was one of my ambi-
tions to learn to be at home in any environment.
Whether a wealthy home or a poverty-stricken one,
whether an American culture or the culture of some
other group, I wanted to be able to live in that environment as though I had grown up in it. This ambition was no doubt laudable and its attainment is very
useful to the missionary. I found later, however, that
it does not quite go to the heart of the problem. My
ambition at present is not so much to be able to live
happily in any *environment* as to be able to live happily with any other *missionary*.

This statement may horrify some of my readers.
If I had said I make it my ambition to be able to live
happily with anyone, you would have had no bone to
pick with me. But no, I *must* say, *with any other missionary!* Am I trying to imply that some missionaries
are hard to live with? That class of God's devoted
servants who have given up all to go for Him to the
far corners of the earth? Let anyone else be hard to
get along with, but surely not missionaries!

Well, missionaries (excepting some feeble folk
like me) are the salt of the earth. At the same time,
my experience on the foreign field leads me to the
conclusion that it takes a good deal more grace to live

happily with one's fellow workers on the foreign field
than it does at home. Why? The reasons are varied.
I think I can safely say that most missionaries are
rather strong-minded. If they were not, perhaps they
would never have gotten to the foreign field! They
know what they want to do, and they know how they
want to do it. Most missionaries will agree on the
task to be accomplished; but what are the best means
to accomplish it—that is not always so easy to agree
upon! The older worker may think the younger worker's plans wild and impracticable. The younger worker may think the older worker stodgy and in a rut.
Perhaps both may be right. Happy the fellow workers
who can learn to discuss their pet ideas without heat!
Happy the fellow workers who can develop just the
right combination of initiative and co-operation!

It is hard to realize how closely one is shut up to
a fellow worker on the mission field. Probably there
are no others of your own race in the place where
you live. At home one can live with one group, work
with another, and have special friends that are entirely
apart from either group. On the field there is no one
else—no one who speaks your native tongue, understands your background, or has the same pattern of
thought as yourself. Perhaps you are stationed with
one other worker. Every human heart longs for some
special friend; but this fellow worker may not be one

you would have chosen for a special friend. Perhaps she has some mannerisms that are irritating to you. Perhaps you like dogs and she hates them. Perhaps she believes in being extremely economical and you like to spend money more freely. In some ways, as two single missionaries live and work together, the relation is as close as that between husband and wife; but in this case the two *have not chosen one another.* Of course the relationship is not established for life; and the missionary who finds herself paired off with an uncongenial fellow worker may console herself by hoping that a change will come soon. That frame of mind, however, is not exactly conducive to the sort of adjustment that would make for the most effective carrying on of the work.

Even married couples will feel this to a certain extent. A young married couple will probably have to live with an older couple for the first two or three years on the field. Owing perhaps to the shortage of men, and perhaps to other reasons, it even happens that sometimes a young married couple is sent to live for their "breaking-in" period with one or two older single lady missionaries! The initial period passes, and they are given a home and a work of their own. But they are not likely to be left alone long. Younger workers will be coming along, and most married couples are rarely without other workers living in their homes. Besides this, it is likely that the husband will need to be away from home for weeks and even months at a time, leaving the wife at home with the little ones and the junior workers.

The single worker feels the force of this even more strongly. Two good friends *may* be placed in a station together; or what is more likely, two who have been placed together may become especially good friends. The fact that they are good friends, however, cannot be a reason for placing them together, nor for leaving them together. Any of us would realize that. The placing of workers is determined by the best interests of the work. If, when the best interests of the work are considered, it seems right to place two special friends together, or to leave them together, well and good. If not, why, that's the end of it!

Not being able to choose my own fellow worker will present two possible difficulties for me. One is that I may be placed with someone who does not appeal to me. The other is that I may be separated from someone with whom I strongly desire to remain. The first difficulty is one that comes along now and then. Probably most missionaries, at one time or another, have had a period of living with someone with whom they did not seem to "hit it off." The second difficulty is, for the unmarried worker at least, of much more common occurrence. Over and over again it happens. Just when you and someone else have lived together long enough to rub off the rough corners, and come to a place where you really "fit," along comes an upheaval, and you are separated. We like to put down roots. We like to make friends and stay with them, but on the mission field frequent change of location and of fellow workers is the normal thing. New personnel is constantly being added, and older workers are constantly retiring. New stations are constantly being opened. And the single worker, time and time again, finds herself being separated from a fellow worker with whom she would prefer to remain permanently!

Some will notice that I have been using pronouns in the feminine gender. This is not without reason, since by far the majority of single workers on the field are women. And, as has been said, one of the hardest things the single woman worker must face is that she can never say to anyone, "I'm going to stay with you."

"What a negative sort of outlook!" exclaims someone; and we must thank that one for reminding us that there is a *positive* side. There is One whom we *may* choose for our Companion. (How amazing that *I* should be allowed to *choose Him!*) And it is just because we have already chosen the one Companion who will not leave us that we may not choose anyone else—not even a husband or wife—without reference to Him. As soon as we choose Him, then He does all our choosing for us.

According to old Oriental custom, marriages were arranged by parents with the aid of a middleman. Sometimes when things went wrong after marriage one of the couple, or both, would blame the middleman. When marriages are made after the Western pattern, there is no one to blame but oneself. Before I left America I used to think that marriages arranged by parents, through middlemen, must necessarily be unhappy. But after I had been on the field for a time I decided that in China the proportion of happy marriages among those outside of Christ was greater than marriages of those of the same group in America, even though almost all the marriages in China were made after the old traditional style! People who choose partners for themselves do not always choose wisely. Older people, with more experience, may make a wiser choice than the young people themselves would have done. It *may* be better to have a trustworthy middleman than to try to do the choosing oneself!

If this is true of an earthly middleman, how much more it is true of the One who chooses for *us!* The earthly middleman may do very well in many cases, but certainly he makes some mistakes. The One who chooses for us makes no mistakes. So whether it be a matter of accepting a fellow worker you would rather not have, or of letting go one whom you would like to keep—remember the One who does the choosing for us makes no mistakes.

CHAPTER 10

The Right to Feel Superior

THE MEETING of the Missionary Union had closed. The Bible Institute students were leaving the room in groups, and many of them were discussing the message which they had just heard.

"What did you think of his last point?" asked one.

"That about race prejudice, you mean? About not thinking that because our skin is white, we're better than anyone else? To tell the truth, it seemed a bit superfluous to me. I suppose race prejudice and race pride still do exist, but not in a group like this. Why, we're practically all missionary candidates!"

"Just what I thought myself!" rejoined the first. "You'd think he'd gotten his audience mixed. But he knew he was talking to missionary candidates, all right. That's the strange part. The rest of his talk— it was the real stuff. But that one point—I just couldn't make it out."

"Oh, he's just fifty years out of date, that's all," commented another. "That's the way it was when *he* went to the field—the imperialistic white man and the downtrodden native—but times have changed.

91

People wouldn't act like that now. Each race has its own culture, and its own contribution to make to enrich the culture of the world. We realize all this now. The Christian world has come a long way since *he* was in training. Pride of race! We're more likely to be ashamed of our race, if he only knew it. Look at the state the world's in—all trouble stirred up by the white race!"

"Some of those old missionaries *were* imperialistic, all right!" A slight, blond youth joined the conversation. "You should hear some of the tales my father tells! Ordering the native people around as if they were slaves! Such cases were few and far between, of course. But, you know, I don't think that's the sort of thing he was driving at. Times may change, but not the human heart. Pride is just as easy a sin to fall into as it ever was. Thinking that we're better than someone else—it may not be because of our race, but merely because the other fellow is poor or uneducated—we can't just dismiss it and say, 'I'm in no danger of that.'"

"Well, perhaps there's something—"

"Aw, just because you grew up on a mission field —"

"You know, *I* think—" Several began to talk at once. Suddenly a gong rang, and the group scattered in all directions.

"Oh, Ann, I've been wanting to find you! A bunch of us are planning to go to Tong's for a Chinese meal. Do you want to come along?"

"Chinese meal? Dear me, I've never had one. Do you have to eat with chopsticks? Don't they serve you rats and mice and all sorts of horrible things?"

"Of course not, you silly! There are the most delicious things! And you don't have to eat with chopsticks unless you want to. In fact, they always give us knives and forks unless we especially ask for chopsticks. But I adore strange ways! This will be my third time for Chinese food. We always ask for chopsticks—it's the most fun trying to use them! Though I must admit that we usually give up halfway—the food is so delicious and we're so hungry we have to. Then you'll come?"

"Well—to tell the truth, I'm afraid it will be some awful stuff I can't eat."

"I'm surprised at you, Ann! You're a missionary candidate, aren't you? You'll *have* to get used to strange—"

"No, but it seems so sort of uncivilized to eat with sticks, or fingers—and all out of one dish, isn't it? Ugh!"

"Now don't be fussy! Didn't you hear that missionary talk last night? You've got to appreciate other people's ways on the mission field—can't go around thinking your ways are best!"

"I know." Ann was suddenly very serious. "But there's only one thing about it that bothers me. What if your own ways really *are* best?"

Chopsticks, or knives and forks—which are best? Not which are the most intriguing, or cause the most hilarity, but which really and truly are the most useful for their purpose—that of conveying food to one's mouth in a convenient and graceful manner. Don't condemn Ann offhand. If I were to ask *you* this question, what answer would *you* give?

"Well—really—" you say. "After all—" Yes. That's just it. You, and Ann, and millions more can't help realizing (or is it feeling?) that your way *is* best. But what about the millions in China and Japan? How would they answer the question? Did you ever stop to think that their reaction would be just as immediate, and their answer just as sure? And I think I am safe in saying that a larger proportion of them have actually tried using the other person's implements than we have.

When a group of ex-China missionaries get together at home and go to a Chinese restaurant for a meal, the first thing they do after ordering is to request that the food be served in bowls, and they be supplied with chopsticks instead of knives and forks. Why? Ask any of them. The reply you will probably get is, "Oh, it doesn't taste the same when eaten with knives and forks!" And the strange part about it is that it is really true.

"But," you say, "chopsticks are so difficult to use!" Not at all! You just need a little practice. Even knives and forks are difficult for beginners to manage. You would know that if you had watched as many beginners (adults) try to use them as I have.

"No, but you can't cut anything with them!" Of course you can't. The kitchen is the place for cutting up food. To serve a slab of meat on a plate, and expect the eater to saw off pieces with a dull knife—it's utterly barbarous! Chinese food is properly prepared, bite-size, in the kitchen.

"Oh? But what about soup or gravy? You can't eat *them* with chopsticks!" Quite true; neither can you eat them with knife and fork. Chinese eat soup with a spoon, or drink it from a bowl.

"Well, chopsticks are awkward, in any case!" Awkward? What are you talking about? They are just like pincers—you nip a bite and pick it up daintily, instead of spearing, or shoveling, as you do with a fork.

It's amazing how hard it is for an American (I won't speak for other nationalities!) to come to the place where he will appreciate the fact that the ways of people in other lands are in many cases better for them than our ways would be. If you are going to the foreign field in order to teach "the American way of life," you had better stay at home. In saying this I do not mean that Americans do not have some skills that it might be advantageous for the people on some foreign mission fields to learn. But any missionary who has the feeling that his ways of doing things are better just because they are "civilized" ways, or "American" ways, or just his own ways, is heading for trouble.

When I first went to China I thought I had no feeling of race superiority. Then an incident occurred that showed me I was not as humble as I had thought. It was at the Chinese New Year season. Chinese New Year is the time of preparing all sorts of special foods, and frequently at that time some of the Christian women would send us a bowl of this, or a plate of that. There was a neighborly feeling about it all that warmed my heart. Then one year a fairly wealthy Christian woman, who had just recently moved to our city, sent her servant over with a gift of a different kind. It was not food this time, but money. In purchasing value the amount would have been equivalent to an American dollar or two. It was the first money gift that had ever been presented to me by a Chinese.

I had always been pleased with the gifts of food, but somehow, when I saw what this gift was, I reacted strongly against it. There was something in me that rebelled. *"I don't need your money!"* was my instinctive reaction. Fortunately I had enough politeness left to realize that I could not refuse it without offending the giver, and so I did take it, mumbling my thanks, which I did not feel, and watched the servant depart. Then I sat down to think it out. *Why* did it make me so uncomfortable to accept that gift? When I finally got to the bottom of it, I decided that the real reason was that I unconsciously felt that it put me in an inferior position. Accepting a gift of food was different—that was just neighborliness. But a small gift of money! That is normally given by a superior to an inferior—a father to his child, a mistress to her servant, one who has sufficient for his needs to one who has not. In this case the giver did not look at it like that, of course. Money gifts were a common thing in her circle, and to her the amount was not too small. But my unconscious reaction was that I was being put in an inferior position, and this was the thing at which I rebelled. How could I, who was this woman's superior (this was my unconscious feeling), take this money, and so accept the place of being her inferior?

The position of a missionary is something like that

of a teacher. He comes to tell people something that they do not know; to introduce a Friend of whom they have not heard. He certainly knows more about Christianity, academically and experimentally, than the people to whom he goes—otherwise there would be no point in his going. He probably knows more about the world in general than the people to whom he goes. He may know better ways of living and working, even for their environment, than they do. How can a person be conscious of how much more he knows than someone else, and still not feel *superior?* Those among whom he works may realize that he knows much that they should learn, and may look up to him as a superior being. This makes it even harder. How can he overcome the superiority complex that comes from race, or from looking on oneself as *civilized,* or even just from recognizing that one has more education and experience than those among whom he works?

The first step in conquering this superiority complex is to realize that it is there. Most of us have it without realizing it. If we realize that this thing probably exists somewhere in our make-up, it will be easier to recognize it when it suddenly rears its head, as it did with me. Seeing it for what it is is the first step in conquering it. The second step, I think, is to become thoroughly acquainted with those to whom we go. Perhaps if we know more about them we will not find them so inferior. Go and live their life with them, twenty-four hours of the day. Don't just put yourself in the position of an observer, but try to do the things that they do. You will probably find that you are not as proficient in doing most of the things that they do as are their ten-year-old children! If your people are *uncivilized,* go into the jungle with them and try to wrest your living from the jungle—try to find or make everything that you need. If they are *civilized,* but poor and backward, go into their homes, and live their lives with them. See how they grow their own food, and that without the use of modern machinery; how they grind their own grain into flour, salt or dry their own vegetables, butcher their own meat—if they have any; how they raise cotton, pick it, card it, spin it, dye it, weave it into cloth, and make the clothes for the family without the aid of a sewing machine. And then watch them (as I often have) make beautiful embroidery for relaxation! By the time you have become really familiar with (I won't say proficient in) their way of life, I think you will have lost most of your feeling of superiority. You will no more think of them as "ignorant savages," or "those from lower cultural groups." Instead, they will just be John, and Mary, and Peter, and Paul— or whatever their names happen to be—real people,

like you and me; real people, who are amazingly skill-
ful in some ways, and amazingly stupid in others,
just like the rest of us.

There is one more thing we need to do in conquering that superiority complex. We need to realize
what a difference having Christ makes. Those to
whom we minister may live in the midst of filth and
disease. Their minds may be dull, and their hearts
dark and full of fears. (Were our ancestors any different when Christ found them?) But see them come
to the One who is the Light of the world, and watch
the transformation that takes place. Then realize
more deeply than ever all that you owe to Christ,
and the greatness of His power in making the one
who comes to Him literally "a new creation." What
these people need is not a training that will educate
them out of their environment. What they need is
not to learn to use knives and forks instead of chopsticks or fingers. What they need is a LIFE that will
transform them, and enable them to live a life of
victory over sin and the Devil within their environment. This imparted life may gradually transform
that environment too—probably it will; but that is
a secondary thing. There is one thing that is essential,
and one alone—the impartation of the life of Christ.
It does not matter how low, how ignorant, how degraded the person is, Christ *is able* to transform him

into someone far superior to me; and it may be that that is *just what He is going to do.* Who am I, a poor redeemed sinner, to look down upon anyone else? Who am I to challenge Christ's power, and refuse to believe that anyone can be made new?

Dear Lord, forgive me for feeling that I am superior to anyone! Open my eyes to see how deep was the pit from which I was digged! Grant that I may make myself one with the people to whom Thou art sending me, and that by faith I can see them transformed by Thy power, even before that transformation has taken place!

CHAPTER 11

The Right to Run Things

A NEW MISSION STATION OPENED! Another conquest of the Gospel! Have you ever wondered how it was done? Suppose you are a missionary, and have already passed successfully through the language-learning stage. Suppose you are assigned an area where the Gospel has never been preached, an area teeming with people, very few of whom have ever even heard the precious name of Jesus. You probably have a fellow worker. You have good health, a reasonable knowledge of the language and local customs, and a heart on fire for God. You have a certain amount of financial resources. What do you do? How do you start in?

Let's see what Mr. Beaver did. When assigned to this new, untouched field, his heart and the heart of his wife were deeply moved. Ten thousand souls and more, and probably not one of them a Christian! Ten thousand souls and more, and it might well be that none of them had ever heard the Gospel preached in any adequate way! Ten thousand souls and more, and the large majority of them had never even heard

the name of Jesus! What an opportunity! What a
challenge!

"Such a challenge calls for action," ruminated Mr.
Beaver. "It calls for immediate action, and yet action
that is well planned, and will be as effective as possible. How can we reach the largest number of souls
for Christ in the shortest time? But what can two people do, anyway? We must have helpers. We must
have a church building, and a native evangelist or
two. We must have a street chapel. We must have a
Christian school, for through it we can reach count-
less numbers of young people. Our church and school
will be established in the central city of the area, of
course. But then, think of all the smaller towns and
villages! As soon as things get going in the city, we
must start outstations in strategic market towns as
well. We must organize tent campaigns, making use
of modern equipment—public address system, re-
cordings, films, and all the rest. We must also start a
social welfare program that will help us to get in
touch with the poorer classes—and aren't the bulk
of the people always poor? A certain amount of relief funds, administered carefully to the deserving,
will make the love of Christ known in a practical way,
and surely will attract folk to our church."

So ran the thoughts of Mr. and Mrs. Beaver, and,
because they were "go-getters," their plans were soon

put into effect. A fine piece of property was pur-
chased. Buildings were erected: a residence for themselves, a preaching hall opening directly on the main
street, fine school buildings, and a beautiful church
building. Crowds of people came to listen to the sing-
ing, to see Christian films, and to hear the Gospel
preached in simplicity and power. It was not long before people were giving their names as inquirers. The
missionaries' servants were among the first to respond,
and their friends and relatives followed. Other helpers around the place were needed: a gardner, a gate-
keeper, and so on, and naturally these were chosen
from among the first converts. Soon the busy compound was like one happy family—all gathering the
first thing in the morning for prayer, and joining
their voices in song, praising the One of whom they
had never heard three months ago, but who now was
their acknowledged Saviour. Callers came from morning till night. Mr. Beaver was never too busy to see
them, to hear their tales of woe, to point them to the
Saviour, and to give them a little judicious help.

"It's not too wise," he thought, "to give out a lot
of money for nothing. I don't want to make paupers
of these people. What they need is jobs, and someone
who will encourage them to work, training them if
necessary. Let's see—I've got quite a bit of relief
funds in hand; and there's plenty of work that needs

to be done to improve this property. So-and-so [one
of the new inquirers] is a builder; I'll put him in
charge of operations, and we'll take on all these poor
people who need help—much better than giving
them help outright—and we'll really put this place
into shape. Not only will our property benefit, but it
will also give these people a chance to hear the Gospel again and again, until they really understand it.
I'm sure that many of them will accept the Lord if
this plan goes through!"

And so things went. Such large numbers gave their
names as inquirers, and they studied and attended
services so faithfully that within six months the first
baptismal service was held. What joy it brought to the
hearts of Mr. and Mrs. Beaver! Two other such services were held before the first year was up, and by
that time Mr. Beaver felt it right to appoint deacons,
and to get the church on an organized basis. He chose
several of the most promising young people, includ-
ing one who had served in his home, and sent them
off to a Bible institute, looking forward with great
joy to the time when they would graduate and come
back to help him in the work. Then he would be able
to let his original evangelists go (they were getting
a bit too bossy anyway, and thought they knew how
the Lord's work should be carried on better than he
did!), and have only his own spiritual children as-

sociated with him in the work. They would all work happily under his direction, and surely the Lord could bless more where the workers were all one in heart. Well, he wouldn't say that these evangelists were *not* one in heart with him, but still—sometimes he felt that there was just a little something lacking. Sometimes they didn't support his plans with all the enthusiasm that they might.

By the time three more years had passed, Mr. Beaver had put up church buildings in six market towns, and was just waiting until his first young people graduated from the Bible institute and came back before starting regular weekly services in the last three of the six towns. He traveled constantly, and wherever he went the people flocked to him for help and advice. True, there were one or two that turned against him, but one couldn't expect the Lord's work always to be easy; and the large majority looked to him as children to a father. There were elders as well as deacons in the church now, and when he presided at their meetings and looked over the group, his own spiritual children now taking their places as leaders in the church, his heart just melted. True, they were a bit hesitant about going ahead, and always consulted him before making plans, but that was only natural and right. After all, they had only a few years' experience in the church and couldn't be expected to know how best to govern the House of God. Indeed, several times he had found it necessary to put his foot down when one of them, a little less experienced and more reckless than the others, had advanced his own ideas of how church affairs should be managed. But he had soon subsided and realized his mistake. What a happy family the church was, indeed, with everything working out just as he had planned it! Truly God was good!

At the time when Mr. Beaver went to his new station and began putting his magnificent plans into effect, another worker was sent, in the same way, to a new area. Mr. Trainer was perhaps not so dynamic an individual, but he knew just as clearly what his plans were for the church that was as yet unborn. "The church, which is his body"—the Body of Christ! The Church which is, through the indwelling Christ, the light of the world! The Church, where each member is in vital contact with the Head, and so, necessarily, is in vital contact with every other member! The Church, each member of which is indwelt by the Holy Spirit, and each member of which feels his responsibility to live and witness for the One who means all in all to him! The church Mr. Trainer wanted to plant was a church which was all this—a church which was a living plant, with its roots going down

into God; a church which did not look to the missionary, or any other man, for its needs, but which was
centered upon Christ; a church which would be given
"gifts" by the Holy Spirit, and would be able to use
those gifts to the edifying of itself, and the bringing
of souls into the kingdom.

Mr. Trainer, like Mr. Beaver, went to the central
city of his area and located on a main street. His
"compound" was a tiny rented house, with a pocket-
handkerchief-size courtyard. He did no building at
all, and his few rooms were sparsely furnished. Books
were the only things he seemed to own. There were
books everywhere, said his callers, but not much else
—some perfectly ordinary furniture, and that was all.
He had no street chapel, and no paid workers brought
in from the outside; but day by day he set a table and
a few stools in his gateway, covered the table with attractive Gospel literature printed in the language of
the people, and there he sat and read. Passersby
stopped to examine his books. One and all received
an attractive Gospel tract, and had the message explained in simple language as long as they cared to
listen. Some bought Gospels and other booklets. A
few got into the habit of dropping by every evening,
when work was done; and Mr. Trainer taught them
to sing Gospel songs and choruses, and read the Word
with them. At other times he went from shop to shop,

giving out tracts, and inviting people to call when
they had time.

The compound of Mr. Trainer was tiny, compared
with that of Mr. Beaver. He had no school, and no
church building. He did not even hold church services at first—who was there to come? Not another
Christian in all that area. He did not attract huge
crowds. He did not spend large sums of money, nor
employ large numbers of people. People did not come
to him for financial assistance—what would be the
use, when he did not seem to have any more money
than anyone else? But he attracted a few, a few
"whose heart the Lord opened," and day by day he
taught them more about the Saviour. It was a full
year before he had a baptismal service. The numbers
baptized were far smaller than those baptized by Mr.
Beaver, but the joy in his heart was just as real.

Even before these converts were baptized, Mr.
Trainer started teaching them about the Church. He
taught them that they were indwelt by the Holy
Spirit. He led them daily to the Throne of Grace,
and from the beginning they learned to pray. He encouraged in them the desire to win others of their
own households and their friends. He encouraged
them to witness, both in their own group, and to those
who did not know Christ. He encouraged them to
bring others to the little evening gathering, and then

to testify in front of these whom they had brought. He did not make too many concrete suggestions, but prayed, and waited for the Holy Spirit to suggest ways and means of witnessing to them. Soon he was invited to their homes to talk to others in their families about the Lord. He always made such occasions an opportunity for the one who invited him there to speak, asking for that one's personal testimony, as well as speaking himself. Sometimes others of the group went along, and they too had a chance to testify. Then it came about quite naturally that the little informal evening meeting was held in the different homes, rather than always in that of Mr. Trainer. Soon different ones were taking turns leading, with spontaneous testimonies, or sharing of "wonderful thoughts" from the Word that came to them in their own private devotions. They would tell about opportunities they had to witness for the Lord, and there would be prayer all around for the requests brought before the group. Soon other souls were coming to the Saviour, not because of the direct efforts of the missionary, but rather through the instrumentality of these young Christians. That, felt Mr. Trainer, was the greatest triumph of all!

Although he was eager to start street meetings, Mr. Trainer did not want this to be his own personal effort, but rather a church effort. So he restrained himself and said nothing, but prayed constantly about the matter. What was his joy when one day one of them asked, "Couldn't we have a meeting somewhere where more people would come, and we could preach the Gospel to them?" When no one seemed to be able to think of a building both suitable and available, he permitted himself to make a suggestion about open-air meetings he had attended. Never having heard of such a thing, some were doubtful, others amazed. He answered questions about how such meetings were run, but made no recommendation. He heard no more about the subject for a week or two, and then suddenly the whole group (who had been consulting together, it seemed) came to him, eager to have an open-air meeting, with his assistance. Careful preparations were made, musical instruments some of them had were requisitioned, and the first street meeting was held. Although no actual decisions for Christ were made, a good crowd listened, and the Christians were so pleased that from that day the open-air meeting became a regular thing.

Trying to witness or bring a short Gospel message in these meetings brought home to the young Christians their need for more Bible study, so a regular Bible study class was instituted two nights a week, instead of the usual meeting for testimony and prayer. At first they concentrated on helping the speakers prepare their messages for the next street meeting. Later they chose a Book of the Bible, or a certain topic, and asked Mr. Trainer to lead them in their study. Notebooks were filled, and practical methods of Bible study became familiar processes, but most of all they learned to look to the Holy Spirit to take the Word given by His own inspiration and interpret it to their hearts.

When the very first ones came to the Lord, Mr. Trainer had suggested that they meet on the Lord's Day. He had usually taken charge of that service himself. By the time there were a dozen or so baptized Christians, he encouraged them to feel that they, like the Jerusalem church in Acts 6, should choose deacons. The group spent much time in prayer, looking to the Lord for His guidance, and when the deacons were actually chosen, all felt that they were not just their own choice, but men chosen by the Holy Spirit. After they were chosen, he turned over all the services to them, and suggested that they take turns in leading the Sunday morning service, and also speaking at that service. He would be glad to take his turn with the others. And so it was carried out.

All this time they had been meeting in the various homes. The inconvenience of unsuitable rooms and never having enough benches had been felt for some time, so when the deacons took over they decided that something must be done about it. Didn't other places have church buildings? Why couldn't they? Some of the group had the idea that there was some kind of a mission or church somewhere that provided money for such things, so off they went to inquire of the missionary. He explained to them clearly that there *were* mission boards that provided funds, in whole or part, for church buildings in many places; but that this did not seem to be the New Testament way, nor was it the way to build a strong local church. "It would be far better," he said, "to meet in a shanty put up by yourselves, than in a beautiful building that cost you nothing." They had several long talks on the subject, and soon all the Christians were deeply concerned. It seemed impossible to out-argue Mr. Trainer. At the same time it seemed even more impossible to do what he thought they ought to do— contribute enough money to build their own church building! Only twelve or fifteen baptized Christians, and several of them women or young people from homes where the head of the house did not believe— what could they do? Mr. Trainer would only counsel them to pray. And pray they did—there seemed to be nothing else they could do. Finally the deacons made a special offering box for gifts for the new church building, and the money began to come in. The gifts were more than they expected; and yet they were but a drop in the bucket compared with what was needed. Time passed, and the fund slowly grew. Suggestions of "church bazaars" and "fun fairs" were made several times (wherever had they heard of such things?). Mr. Trainer counseled against them, but did not feel that he had the authority to forbid. After all, the church was standing on its own feet, and it stood or fell to Christ alone! But he spent much time in prayer, and none of these suggestions was put into effect.

One Sunday an electrifying announcement was made. A wealthy businessman in the city was offering them a suitable piece of property for their building as an outright gift! The Christians redoubled their efforts in giving, and that month they received ten times as much as they had received in any one month before. A church in a city not too far away heard of their efforts, and sent a contribution. Church membership was growing, and all the new believers became interested in giving. Then two of the deacons made a proposal: "Why can't we do most of the work on the building ourselves? That will make it much less expensive!"

The plans needed careful working out, but assistance was given by someone's neighbor, who was a builder, and finally the work started. Many of them put in long hours of back-breaking labor after their

regular work for the day had been completed. Difficulties appeared, but prayer and perseverance pre-
vailed. After the building was started, many more
gifts came in; and great was the rejoicing when the
simple little chapel was at last finished, and used for
its first Sunday morning service! Throngs of interested neighbors and friends turned up for the meeting,
and several of the deacons took turns at preaching.
A guest speaker had also been invited, the pastor of
the church that had sent an unsolicited offering to
help with the building. The meeting went on for
more than two hours, but everyone was happy, and
again and again praises ascended to God for their
own church building!

A couple of years passed. The work of Mr. Beaver
and Mr. Trainer continued as begun. Then suddenly
the country was threatened by war. Worse still, the
missionaries were labeled as "enemy nationals." A
general evacuation took place. Both Mr. Beaver and
Mr. Trainer were due for furloughs; and even if they
had not been, remaining on the field could only bring
harm to the Christians. Both of them gathered up a
few things and departed, escaping from the country
just in time. If they had remained a few days longer,
they would have found themselves in concentration
camps. When they arrived at home, each had a thrill-

ing tale to tell of how God had worked in saving souls and building up His Church, and also of personal deliverance in time of danger. At the end of every message they gave came these words: "Pray for the Christians there. Because of the war, there is no way of getting news from them, and we have heard nothing since we left. Pray that they may be kept true, and that in spite of war and distress, the churches may grow and expand, and that many more souls may be brought to Christ."

The war was over. Friendly relations between countries were again established. Both missionaries had had profitable furloughs: time for rest and spiritual refreshment, and many opportunities to make known the needs, the difficulties, and the triumphs of the mission field. Then—something happened. Both men fully expected to get back to their original fields of work, to see again those dear Christians, their sons and daughters in the Lord—but neither did. Another call came to each, and neither could return to his former field. Others went instead—others who knew little about the history of the stations, or what work had been done there. What did these men find in these two fields? I think you can guess!

Mr. Beaver's station had always been supplied with plenty of money from abroad. By becoming a Chris-

tian a man could obtain a certain amount of relief
money, perhaps a job, or free schooling for his children. Many had learned "the language of Zion" and
had been taken into the church who had never had a
change of heart. When war broke out and the missionary left, the jobs were finished, and the school
closed down. There was no one to pay the evangelists,
and they gradually drifted away to other places or into
secular jobs. The deacons and elders had been accustomed to taking orders from Mr. Beaver and had had
no real experience in looking after things themselves.
Even some of those leaders were of the group that had
joined the church, not because they had really re-
pented and turned to Christ, but for the material
benefits they could get.

As soon as Mr. Beaver left, they quarreled among
themselves as to which one would take his place and
be the "big chief." There was no one capable of taking services, because such things had always been in
the hands of Mr. Beaver and his paid workers, who
now were gone. None of the elders or deacons had
ever preached a sermon in his life. Some tried, but
their efforts did not draw the crowds, and attendance
soon dwindled to almost nothing. Then quarrels
about the property began. True, it belonged not to
them, but to the mission board; but surely it was up
to the church to look after it while the missionary was

gone! Several so-called Christian families moved into the empty buildings, with or without the agreement of the deacons and elders; but then, thought they, the buildings *should* be occupied, and of course these people will pay us rent! (They never did.) Church services gradually ceased. A few faithful Christians remained true to the Lord, and met in a home for occasional services; but since none had been trained to lead meetings, all they could do was sing, read the Bible, and pray.

But what had happend at the other station? There the case was far different. They had gone through the sorrows of war, but they had done so with the Lord at their side. Continuing the work of the church was no problem—they had been doing it themselves all along. Money was hard to get, and many young men had to go to war; but the hearts of the people were open as never before, and they had baptisms once and again. They missed Mr. Trainer very much; but they were driven more than ever to the Lord, and found Him sufficient for their every need.

It is easy to say that one man was right and the other was wrong. But how many of us would not have followed in the footsteps of Mr. Beaver if we had not been warned? And how many of us missionaries today, even though warned, are not still in dan-

ger of making ourselves the little center around which
the mission station revolves?

"It's all very well to say that the Christians should
take the responsibility from the very beginning," we
think; "but *here* it is impossible. These people are
too poor! And they are too ignorant! No, they certainly would do everything wrong if I let them take
the lead!" And so we go on telling everyone what he
ought to do, and seeing that he does it; and in the
eyes of the young believers the Christian life becomes
simply a matter of doing what the missionary says.

That is not the way that Paul built churches. Great
and dynamic character that he was, he so taught and
led his groups of young Christians that when after a
few months or a year or two he left them they were
able to carry on by themselves, and even to grow. He
did not put up church buildings for them, nor schools,
nor give them "grants." He brought them to the
place where they could function as living churches, in
direct union with the Head, and not centered upon
himself. His efforts were directed to building up
churches that would be able to stand alone, because
they stood in the strength of the One who upheld
Paul.

Why is it so easy for us missionaries to think that
we know how to do the work of the Lord better than
any mission field convert, especially if that one has

been led to the Lord by us? Doing the Lord's work is
not fundamentally a matter of knowledge, training,
or even experience. It may be true that I have had
years of Bible training, and the little old woman with
whom I am going out visiting has never been to any
sort of school a day in her life; that I have traveled
around the world, and she has never been thirty miles
from the place where she was born; that I have heard
the Gospel and studied the Bible all my life, and she
has known it for only a few short years. I was born
again twenty-five or thirty years ago; she has been the
Lord's own for three or four years. Suppose we go to
call on someone who is ill or in trouble. I get out a
poster, and carefully explain the Gospel. The woman
we are visiting listens to me with her mouth open;
and after twenty minutes of as clear and simple
preaching as I am capable of, when I am just getting
to my climax, she lays her hand on my sleeve and asks
earnestly, "Did you make this dress yourself?"

My heart sinks to my boots. Is that what she has
been thinking about all this time? Is that why she
fixed her eyes on me so intently? What's the use
anyway?

Then the old lady who is with me starts in. *She*
can't even tell clearly the bare outlines of the life of
our Saviour; but she turns to the woman, one whose
life and thoughts she knows (wasn't she just like her

before she was saved?), and says, "Look at me! I used to have this trouble and that trouble and the other trouble, and then I came to Jesus, and asked Him to forgive my sins. He did it and took all my troubles away, and gave me peace and joy in my heart as I never dreamed of. Come to Him and you can have it too!"

When the one on whom we are calling says suddenly, "I'm going to believe too," it is far more likely to be the result of my companion's testimony than of my fine Gospel message!

Are you a missionary volunteer? When you get to the mission field, remember that a simple, earnest testimony from one who is "just like we are" will usually bring far more in the way of results than your own best efforts. Don't think that the missionary is the only one who can bring souls to the Lord. The one who has just been saved may, easily become a more effective witness than you yourself.

No matter how uneducated and degraded the group, there are always in it one or more who are leaders. No matter how poor and ignorant he is, the one who has been truly saved, and knows that he is saved, is always capable of witnessing to others of his own group. No matter how poor a little group of Christians is, if they continue in prayer and patient effort they will surely be able to provide for themselves a meeting house that is as good as their own homes, or a little better. The Church of God is not dependent upon Gothic arches and stained glass windows, upon ministers in Geneva gowns and upon robed choirs. It is not dependent upon material resources, or this world's learning. None of these things are essentials. The only things that are essentials to the Church of Christ are found in Christ and in the penitent and forgiven soul, no matter what his race or culture or economic status. The Church of Christ can function on any level at which men for whom Christ died are living.

It is very easy for the missionary to become a little "pope." God forbid that we should do this! God forbid that we should consider ourselves the exclusive channels for bringing God's grace to needy souls, or the only ones capable of hearing God's voice! God forbid that we should forget that every believer, as soon as he is born again, is indwelt by the Holy Spirit! And may God open our eyes to ways and means of doing what is perhaps the greatest task of the missionary, the task of bringing the young church to the place where it can get along without us, the task of working ourselves out of a job!

CHAPTER 12

He Had No Rights

He had no rights:

No right to a soft bed, and a well-laid table;

No right to a home of His own, a place where His own pleasure might be sought;

No right to choose pleasant, congenial companions, those who could understand Him and sympathize with Him;

No right to shrink away from filth and sin, to pull His garments closer around Him and turn aside to walk in cleaner paths;

No right to be understood and appreciated; no, not by those upon whom He had poured out a double portion of His love;

No right even never to be forsaken by His Father, the One who meant more than all to Him.

His only right was silently to endure shame, spitting, blows; to take His place as a sinner at the dock; to bear my sins in anguish on the cross.

He had no rights. And I?

A right to the "comforts" of life? No, but a right to the love of God for my pillow.

A right to physical safety? No, but a right to the security of being in His will.

A right to love and sympathy from those around me? No, but a right to the friendship of the One who understands me better than I do myself.

A right to be a leader among men? No, but the right to be led by the One to whom I have given my all, led as is a little child, with its hand in the hand of its father.

A right to a home, and dear ones? No, not necessarily; but a right to dwell in the heart of God.

A right to myself? No, but, oh, *I have a right to Christ.*

All that He takes I will give;
All that He gives will I take;
He, my only right!
He, the one right before which all other rights
    fade into nothingness.
I have full right to Him;
Oh, may He have full right to me!